THE

BIOLOGICAL, SOCIOLOGICAL

AND

PSYCHOLOGICAL ASPECTS OF AGING

The Biological,
Sociological
and Psychological
Aspects of Aging

By

KURT WOLFF, M.D.

Clinical Director
Galesburg State Research Hospital
Galesburg, Illinois
Formerly, Director of Geriatric
Treatment and Research Unit
Osawatomie State Hospital
Osawatomie, Kansas

GREENWOOD PRESS, PUBLISHERS
WESTPORT, CONNECTICUT

Library of Congress Cataloging in Publication Data

Wolff, Kurt, 1907-
    The biological, sociological, and psychological
aspects of aging.

    Reprint of the ed. published by C. C. Thomas,
Springfield, Ill.
    Bibliography: p.
    1. Aged. 2. Aged--Psychology. I. Title.
[HQ1061.W6 1978]   301.43'5   78-6601
ISBN 0-8371-9057-6

Reprinted with the permission of Charles C. Thomas,
Publisher

Reprinted in 1978 by Greenwood Press, Inc.,
51 Riverside Avenue, Westport, CT. 06880

Printed in the United States of America

10 9 8 7 6 5 4 3 2 1

To My Wife

CONTENTS

		Page
INTRODUCTION	....	3
THE BIOLOGICAL ASPECT	....	6
THE SOCIOLOGICAL ASPECT	....	28
THE PSYCHOLOGICAL ASPECT	....	54
REFERENCES	....	85

Kurt Wolff, M.D.

THE

BIOLOGICAL, SOCIOLOGICAL

AND

PSYCHOLOGICAL ASPECTS OF AGING

INTRODUCTION

WHILE child psychiatry has been studied in an organized way since 1909, geriatric psychiatry has been started comparatively recently. With a steadily increasing life expectancy of our population—which was only 48 years in 1900 and 69.8 years in 1956—and the ever enlarging number of patients in the older age group in our state institutions, this lack of organized study in geriatric psychiatry presents a very serious problem.

We have good textbooks by *Stieglitz* (106) and by *Thewlis* (110) and an interesting book published by *Kaplan* (61), but we know as yet very little about the important problem of aging. We need to ask ourselves why are so few psychiatrists interested in such a great psychiatric problem? The number of aged patients in need of treatment and rehabilitation is surely much greater than the number of children in need of psychiatric help. One of the reasons might be that most psychiatrists do not believe that much can be done on the psychiatric side of the geriatric problem, especially in regard to treatment. *Fenichel* (25), a well-known psychoanalyst, stated that the personality structure in an individual over 45 years of age is too rigid to make psychotherapy effective. Insight, said Fenichel, is no longer possible, and memory defects make the psychotherapeutic effort rather difficult. Following this idea, there was a feeling of hopelessness prevailing among psychiatrists.

"We cannot help elderly people," they thought, and concentrated their therapy on children and younger adults. Furthermore, there were countertransference feelings. Many psychiatrists had not worked through their Oedipus complex completely and unconsciously hated the father or mother figure in their patients and became, eventually, too much or too little involved. Modern psychiatry, however, now begins to see more clearly the importance and the urgency of the geriatric problem.

Since 1940, many Institutes of Gerontology have made special studies on the biological aspects of the problem. Gerontological study centers are in existence at Kansas University Medical Center (Kansas), in St. Louis (Missouri), in Iowa City (Iowa), in Bethesda (Maryland), to name only the most outstanding ones, and their work has considerably increased our knowledge on aging as a biological process. But aging has not only a biological aspect; it has its sociological and psychological sides and represents a rather complex and more universal problem. The time has come when we cannot overlook its importance any more and the recent conferences of the American Medical Association give evidence that aging may become the most important problem of our medical world in the future. It appears to me that to solve this problem eventually or even to advance our knowledge further, pathologists, physiologists, internists, psychologists, psychiatrists, sociologists and even politicians must work together in the common interest in order to advance science and to benefit our physically sick or emotionally disturbed elderly population.

I gratefully acknowledge my indebtedness to all those who directly or indirectly have aided me in my efforts, especially to the following who have been a source of inspiration and encouragement:

KARL A. MENNINGER, M.D.

WILLIAM C. MENNINGER, M.D. and

HAROLD E. HIMWICH, M.D.

I wish also to express my sincere thanks to:

THOMAS T. TOURLENTS, M.D. Superintendent, and

ALBERT KORATSKY, D.D.S. of Galesburg Research Hospital for reading the manuscript and much of the other details contingent thereto.

KURT WOLFF.

Galesburg, Ill.
March, 1959.

THE BIOLOGICAL ASPECT

VARIOUS biological factors contribute to the senile changes. According to some investigators, genetic factors are involved. Senescence depends on progressive morphogenic changes, which are not "inherent" properties. Experiments done with animals prove this theory, for instance, offspring from young mothers live longer than those from old. Furthermore, there is an increase of longevity cumulative over successive generations. Matings between long-lived mice have shown that longevity is a characteristic, determined in part by parental influences. Longevity depends also on the species. Reptiles and fish increase in size during their total life span. In contrast, warm-blooded animals grow rapidly during early life and then decline in size after maturity. The length of life depends as well on body temperature. When the body temperature of insects is held slightly elevated, they die earlier than cold-blooded animals, which maintain a uniform temperature. Furthermore, life is shortened by overfeeding in silk worms, rats and mice, while restriction of caloric intake extends their life span. In recent years, increased interest has been shown concerning the effect of radiation on the life span. It has been found that sublethal doses of radiation, for instance, resulted in premature aging in rats.

What actually is the aging process in our organs and tissues? To this question quite a few scientists have given many years of study. The results of these studies can be summarized in the following findings. Aging produces:

1. An increase in connective tissue in the organism.
2. A gradual loss of elastic properties of connective tissue.
3. A disappearance of cellular elements in the nervous system.
4. A reduction of the number of normally functioning cells.
5. An increased amount of fat.
6. A decrease in oxygen utilization.
7. A decrease in the amount of blood pumped, by the heart, under resting conditions.
8. A lesser amount of air expired by the lungs than in a younger organism.
9. A decreased muscular strength.
10. The excretion of hormones, especially by sex glands and the adrenal glands is lower than normal.

Another factor, to which many biologists have given much thought, is the higher incidence of arteriosclerosis in populations where the fat content of the diet is high, a fact which is conducive to reduction of fat in the diet as protection against arteriosclerosis. It seems, however, that in the development of arteriosclerosis saturated fats from animal sources play a greater role than unsaturated fats from vegetables. According to statistics given by insurance companies, overweight in adults definitely reduces life expectancy. Inadequate intake of proteins, minerals and vitamins also appear to be an important factor in reducing our life span. Due, perhaps, to poor dentition, old people are apparently more prone to consume a higher amount of carbohydrates.

Sex is a striking factor in longevity. A constant feature

has been the higher degree of survivorship for females at any age group. *Lewis* (74) has found pronounced female survivorship after the age of 50. Twenty years from now, women may exceed men by 10% in the older age group after 65.

The majority of gerontologists agree that a sharp distinction should be made between the process of aging and the state of being aged that is senility. *Lansing* (70) considers senescence to be a process of progressive loss for the adult of the ability to live, while senility is a state of adulthood in which the ability to live has been reduced. After the age of 40, *Lansing* points out, the individual is prone to accumulate fat, the physical capacities are reduced, vision is deteriorating and there is a lack of adaptability to environmental changes. The elderly person has learned to compromise. He fatigues more easily and does not generally force issues. While mortality, due to infections, has considerably decreased in old age, chronic rheumatic- and osteo-arthritis, cardiovascular disease, cancer, and diseases of the nervous system become predominant and represent a serious problem of treatment and rehabilitation. Yet, problems connected with aging can and do occur in young adulthood. Arteriosclerosis is not solely limited to advanced age, and calcification of the aorta can, indeed, begin at the age of 20. Other investigators believe that age pigments are an important characteristic of the process of aging, but already at the age of 7 the first traces of yellow pigment can be observed in several types of nerve cells in men. They can be found in the liver, the adrenal glands, the cardiac muscle, the anterior pituitary glands and nerve cells. Acid-fast age pigments appear frequently in human cardiac muscle as soon as the age of 20 and increase thereafter. *Lansing* (69) believes that calcium may play an important role in establishing the aging process because calcium lowers cell permeability.

Gerard (31) relates the phenomena of aging especially to the nervous system. According to *Gerard,* slower learning, greater rigidity in what one "knows," less willingness to shift views, decrease of recent memory and quantitative loss of sensory acuity, as well as a loss of motoric speed and power are conducive to the factor of aging. Neurons decrease in size, the metabolic rate is slowed down, the cells carry more slag and decay and there is an accumulation of calcium which slows the function of the cells. In this way, further fiber and dendrite growth becomes impossible. Aging, as defined by *Gerard,* is a failure of the regenerative, reconstitutive and rejuvenative process.

Himwich, H. E. and *Himwich, W. A.* (51) give much importance to the fact that after 40 years of age the basal metabolic rate or the oxygen consumption of the entire body gradually falls, with a more rapid rate decrease after 80 years of age. The *Himwichs* have observed a gradual increase of water at the expense of solid elements in old age, the metabolism of the brain declines with the basal metabolism and the brain appears to shrink. *Buerger* (3) found a definitive decrease of the size of the brain after the age of 30. *Heinrich* (49) pointed out that, while the ventricles of the brain enlarge in old age and the total volume of cerebrospinal fluid increases, the brain tissue itself contracts. The *Himwichs* find both the white and the gray matter of the cerebral cortex show an accumulation of moisture in old age, and believe that the gradual increase of water at the expense of solid elements, along with morphological alterations may represent the basis for mental impairment of the elderly. Very interesting are the studies of *Buerger* (4) in regard to the chemical changes of the brain substance in old age. He comes to the conclusion that there is a definitive decrease of the total brain lipids from 78 to 90 years. Generally, the amount of proteins, and especially the values of glutamic acid, glutamine pyruvic acid and alpha-keto glutamic acid in the brain tissue diminish. Furthermore, *Nikitin's* and his co-workers (90) studies suggest that protein, although decreasing in quantity, remains unchanged as to its amino acid content.

It is a fact, however, that the regressive changes in the brain substance itself are not always associated with clinical manifestations. The question as to why the decreased metabolism, due to augmented cerebral vascular resistance and dependent on retardation of blood flow, is not compensated by reduction of cerebral vascular resistance when the blood pressure falls, cannot as yet be answered. Therefore, many authors believe that besides the parenchymal damage which causes alteration in the brain cells, still another factor must be present which causes the phenomenon of aging. This could be some kind of toxic product of still unknown origin, influencing the function not only of our brain cells but of the cells of our organism as a whole. Experiments, then, done during recent years, by the *Himwichs* (52), suggest that generally, in old age, nitrogen and phosphorus substances decrease in the brain, while sulfur rich substances increase at the age of 90. The lipid and total protein fractions decline and some "undefined lipid," perhaps the lipochrome of the yellow plaques is augmented. The cells and axons of the central nervous system dwindle, the aqueous element of the brain expands. Ventricles enlarge and the brain shows parenchymal atrophy. *Kety* (65, 66) affirms these findings and states the loss of neurons, the progressive deterioration of certain essential cellular components and the decrease in neuronal interconnections and interactions are important factors, inducing the process of aging. Cerebral oxygen consumption, according to *Kety*, expressed as ml. of oxygen utilized per 100 g. of brain substance per minute, shows a gradual fall with advancing years. For *Kety*, the rapid fall in the circulation and oxygen supply for the brain from childhood to aging is at the base of all the other chemical, biological and functional changes.

Lowry and *Hastings* (80) observed that extreme age results in an increase in water, sodium and chloride and a decrease in acid-soluble phosphorus and potassium in the skeletal muscle. Interpreted histochemically, age has resulted in a near doubling of the extracellular fluid without change in water or potassium concentration in the cell. The moderate increase in lipid concentration is of interest, since like the change in extracellular fluid, the change with old age is the reverse of the change with growth. There is a suggestion that the extracellular compartment contains a lower proportion of solids in old age. In general, then, in aging as in growth, the muscle undergoes definite alterations but the composition of the intracellular phase changes comparatively little.

Atrophy is commonly considered an attribute of many old tissues. The skeletal muscle, for example, in a very old individual is greatly reduced in mass, in comparison to its bulk, at the height of vigor. It is not entirely clear, how much of this decrease in total mass is due to actual loss of fibers, and how much is to be accounted for by a decrease in their average size. Extensive measurements demonstrate the ocurrence of hypertrophy in the surviving fibers of the ocular muscles in the 8th and 9th decades, but these studies were purposely made on the eye muscles in which activity is not greatly restricted in old age. It is reasonable to believe that the fibers of larger leg muscles, for instance, undergo considerable atrophy of disuse in later life.

Shock (103) confirms the importance of the decreased basal metabolism in old persons. Reduction in total metabolism is simply a reflection of the reduced number of metabolizing units (cells) present in the organism of the elderly person. Decreased skeletal muscle efficiency, decreased muscle tone, and actual muscle atrophy are, *Shock* suggests, a consequence of advancing age. This concept of decreased metabolic processes of our body cells with advancing age becomes evident by partial involution of the thyroid gland in old age. Dryness of the skin and scalp, loss of hair, lowered resistance to infections, weakness and atony of the skeletal muscles, reduce speed of mental performance and slower reaction time gives proof of it.

The same author (102) made interesting observations on the homeostatic mechanisms* in the aging body. According to this author, the internal temperature of elderly persons is maintained within the same limitations as that in young (under resting or basal conditions). Skin temperature only is slightly lower in older persons than in young subjects due, chiefly, to the diminished circulation in the skin of the aged. There is evidence, however, that the response to high or low environment temperature is less effective in the old than in the young. While young persons show little change in rectal temperature, in aged people a fall of 0.5-1.0° C. during exposure is frequent. It is generally believed that aged individuals show a greater increase in oxygen consumption than the young. They reveal impairment in their ability to adjust to increased environmental temperatures, demonstrated by heat prostration, which happens more frequently among the old than among the

* Cannon defines homeostasis as a term to designate maintenance of a steady state of equilibrium of the cellular environment throughout the body.

young. It is well known that the death rate from heat stroke increases considerably after the age of 60. Furthermore, in elderly subjects, there is less increase in pulse rate than in the young, during the influence of heat, and the ability to dissipate excess heat is lowered. Partial disappearance of skin capillaries, atrophic, dry, rough and unelastic skin, with reduced capacity of the skin capillaries to dilate, is the cause of it. Many studies have been made in regard to blood pressure elevation in old age. According to *Shock,* under conditions of standardized exercise, which does not represent all-out exertion for younger subjects, the increment of blood pressure is significantly greater for old than for young.

Robinson (97) found that the pulse-rate does not increase after exercise in older persons as fast as in younger ones, because the elasticity of the arterial walls is decreased with age. Impairments of the cardiovascular system in old age include slowing of the circulation, which results from a reduction in cardiac output. Many deaths are caused by failure of the circulation.

Gastric disturbances, of various kinds, and kidney dysfunction is rather frequent in old age. The kidneys are damaged by a decrease in number of functional units as well as by changes in their vascular supply. The healing and repair processes of all tissues of the body show that our organism's homeostatic equilibrium fails in old age.

Cancer occurs more frequently. As has been previously pointed out by the author (116) in a paper on the origin of cancer growth, it is a fact that circulatory disturbances leading to venous stasis of the blood with the resultant lack of oxygen is one of the factors not to be overlooked in the etiology of cancer. Maybe circulatory deficiencies, so frequent in old age, are at the bottom of the well known predisposition for cancer, in this age group, and should merit more consideration in regard to treatment and prevention of this disease.

Furthermore, it is well known that aged patients reveal a greater sensitivity to all kinds of drugs. For instance, the author has observed that agranulocytosis and leukopenia occur more frequently and much faster in the older age group after the use of tranquilizers. Drugs can be prescribed in quantitatively smaller dosages for the geriatric patient than those prescribed for younger adults (117).

It appears also, that the amount of antibodies, agglutinins, and precipitins in the blood is decreased in the older age groups. It is a well known fact that the functional properties of the sexual organs diminish in old age. Furthermore, the sensory apparatus of the whole organism is in decline. Visual acuity is reduced, partially due to either physiological hyperopia in old age, glaucoma, cataracts, or damage to the retina of the eye. Impairment of hearing, especially for high pitched sounds, can be due to otosclerosis, and occurs frequently.

Muscular tone, coordination of the muscular system, and speed of muscular movement frequently show alterations or impairments. In most organs, cells are substituted by connective tissues causing either defective function, atrophy or other degenerative changes.

Stieglitz (107) is of the opinion that one of the most important contributions of modern medicine was a conceptual clarification concerning the child as not merely "a little man," but as an organism which presents structural, functional, chemical, metabolic, nutritional and psychological characteristics peculiar to his biological age. In a similar way, old people, too, are structurally, functionally and mentally different persons than they have been in younger years. *Stieglitz* is in favor of a special approach to the geriatric problem which considers structural, functional and chemical changes by themselves. The structural changes involve an atrophy of parenchymatous tissues and in consequence, an increase in interstitial tissue. This does not mean, however, that structural changes are always associated with functional impairment. The normal functional reserves are very great and are not exhausted easily. Naturally, renal, hepatic, pancreatic, or thyroid atrophy affects the whole organism. Histological and histochemical studies of the individual tissue cells alone do not resolve the problem regarding the origin of senility. Cellular proliferation declines with old age and necrocytosis (atrophy of cells resulting in their death) increases. Functional changes concerning the pulse rate, arterial tension, body temperature, and water content are an indication of an altered equilibrium. In regard to speed of response and effectiveness, the aged have more difficulty in maintaining a uniform body temperature and tolerating cold. Perhaps, due to partial atrophy of the sweat glands, they are more sensitive to a hot environment.

It is well known that either increased intake or deprivation of sugar is badly tolerated by elderly persons. An imbalance in the hydrogen-ion concentration of the blood frequently gives rise to serious disturbances because the homeostatic equilibrium of the organism, in the older person, is more easily disturbed and returns to its normal level with more difficulty.

Whether the degeneration of cells and tissues is due, more or less, to overwork and abuse, or whether senescence and atrophy is to be attributed rather to disuse and lack of work, remains open to discussion. It seems to me that neither theory can be neglected and both are worthy of consideration. Apparently then, abuse and disuse could cause senile changes and should be given importance in relation to the individual organism and the individual person involved.

Freeman (28) has given special consideration to the factor of endocrine mechanisms in the aging body. This author observed evidence that the pituitary-adrenal mechanism responds with average expectancy, even in the very old. In a study of adreno-cortical response to adreno-cortiocotropic hormone (ACTH) in young and old men, it was found that there may be a decrease in ACTH production with age. Furthermore, it has been shown in humans that the production of gonadotropin is greater in aging women than in young ones, and that hypophysical changes are not marked in senescence. In the thyroid gland, however, the uptake of radio-isotopic iodine is decreased with age. In older men there is usually a decrease in the concentration of serum proteinbound iodine (PBI), which is less marked in women. The parathyroid glands were found to be very resistant to changes associated with aging. On the other hand, the pancreas appears to be more susceptible to changes in elderly persons. Deficiency of the pancreas in the production of insulin induces to a decreased glucose tolerance of the diabetic type. Significant modifications in adreno-cortical response could not be revealed. In older men, according to *Freeman,* no diminished adreno-cortical activity under ACTH stimulation, whether in degree, duration, metabolic as hematologic effects, has been demonstrated. Most scientists, working on this field, appear to agree that gonadal failure has remained the only endocrine alteration characteristic of old age, and the ovary may be completely worn out and unable to respond to specific pituitary stimulation. Therefore, it is generally believed that, in the aging body, there is a persistence of the integrity of the pituitary-adrenal mechanism; there is maintenance of the functional capacity of the catabolism-mediating glands in contrast to a progressive loss of capacity in the glands with anabolic activities; and there is a definite reduction in the biological and chemical reserves by which anabolic effects can be accomplished.

Selye (101) stresses the factor of close interrelations between the "general adaptation syndrome" and aging. This author believes that older people can, at first, get used to the alarming effects of cold, heavy muscular work, worries and so on. Although, after prolonged exposure, sooner or later all resistance breaks down and exhaustion sets in. Something gets lost or used up during the work of adaptation. Energy is consumed in the process of adaptation. This energy is completely different from the caloric energy we get by eating. Although we do not know exactly what this energy might be, research along these lines could advance investigation into the fundamentals of aging. This adaptation energy depends to a great extent on our genetic background. We are able to draw thriftily upon this energy reserve for a long, but monotonously uneventful, existence or we can spend it lavishly in the course of a stressful, intense, more colorful and exciting life. Rest cannot restore lost energy for people after exposure to very stressful activities, entirely. Reserves of adaptability cannot be completely replaced and each exposure to stress leaves scars which influence our life. Aging, according to *Selye,* is due to a deficit in adaptation energy during life. Nobody, this author states, ever dies of old age because all the organs of the body wear out and wreck the whole human machinery in consequence. This seems to be the price human beings pay for the evolution from a simple cell into a highly complex organism. Unicellular animals never die, because they divide and their parts live on.

According to the investigation of *Kallmann* (58), genetic

factors may be largely responsible for the physical and mental disorders in the presenile period of life. A study of heredity has, therefore, great influence; as it helps us reach a better understanding of the prepsychotic personality of senile disturbances, including schizoid personality traits and a tendency to compulsive thinking. A careful study of genetic factors may help us to better understand physical ills prevalent in old age, like cancer, chronic pulmonary tuberculosis, and specific metabolic dysfunctions. Heredity appears to be an important factor in longevity generally, and, specifically, in certain psychoses of old age associated with vascular and metabolic changes. There is no doubt of a positive correlation between the life spans of parents and their children.

Kallmann (57) divides the heredity influences on senescence into three categories. The first group is due to gene-controlled deficiency states, physical or mental, which arise before the senescence period, but alter the "adaptive plasticity" of aging persons. To this group belong the major psychoses, specific metabolic disorders, and various types of subnormal intelligence, emotional instability, schizoid personality traits and compulsive drinking patterns. In most of these conditions the genetic components tend to complicate the process of aging. Not much is known about the cause of failure in adaptive defenses in elderly patients of this kind. The second group is composed of gene-specific disorders limited to the senium, including Pick's, Alzheimer's and Jacob-Creutzfeldt's Diseases. In these sicknesses, which are conducive to gross or relatively circumscribed brain lesions, the hereditary factor might be a specific factor in their development, a theory proven in Pick's Disease, which is caused by a simple dominant gene. It appears also that hereditary factors are of importance for patients suffering from essential hypertension, cerebral arteriosclerosis, and senile dementia. *Kallmann* considers also the influence of hereditary factors on the specific disturbance of the lipid metabolism (primary hypercholesterolemia), which permits early vascular changes. However, hereditary predisposition can hardly be the only, or the most important, factor in early arteriosclerosis. Senile psychoses may be better understood by taking into account many factors leading to an emotional maladjustment before senescence, rather than a single hereditary factor.

A third group exists which has a more or less specific hereditary component with respect to longevity and general survival. To this group belongs a more or less unspecific degree of hereditary influence regarding the age factor of the parents. In addition, the obvious similarities in regard to the physical and mental process of aging, social adjustment, intelligence, and its rate of decline in identical twins are found in this third group.

Ma and *Cowdry* (81) made important studies on aging of the human skin and concluded that, in contrasting the dermal elastic tissue of biopsy specimens of skin of a group of 11 young male adults, of age range 19 to 32 with those of a group of 8 senile males, of age range 78 to 94, marked differences were observed. These included in the latter a decrease in the amount of elastic tissues, which was more evident in the subepidermal elastic plexus than in the deep fiber layer. In the subepidermal plexus a splitting of elastic fibers into component fibrils was observed, which is consistent with the idea that the material, binding them together, was loosened. In the tissue fluid, between both superficial and deep fibers, a cloudiness and a lack of optimal clarity, was seen, which may be correlated with a decrease in permeability.

Cowdry (17) expresses the idea that lesions of the brain or the body in geriatric patients are not due, entirely, to advancing age. In elderly women, for instance, hyalinized and occluded uterine vessels can be canalized and restored to function by administration of estrogen. Pathological findings of the retina in patients suffering from hypertension can be changed to normal ones when the hypertension decreases. In this connection, a paper, published by *Kountz* (67), is of special interest. *Kountz* has found that the nasal mucous membrane in elderly women, which has undergone squamous metaplasia can be restored to its normal condition by estrogen therapy. It is a well-known fact that fatty deposits in the arterial walls of experimental animals can be removed by dietary administration of unsaturated fats.

Therefore, it can be assumed that many pathological processes in old age can be reversed by adequate treatment. Prevention also must be considered, and a too pessimistic viewpoint regarding treatment of geriatric patients is therefore unjustified. Perhaps, in the not too distant future, we will be able to do for the physically ill and emotionally disturbed geriatric patient as much as we are now doing for the child. In fact, the geriatric problem appears of even greater importance and urgency.

Of very great importance for understanding the aging process is the dietary problem. *Stare* (105) has made extensive studies of nutrition and has come to the conclusion that the need for a sound nutrition in the elderly differs only slightly from that in the younger adults. A good dietary plan for the elderly should include fewer calories.

This investigator found a mean caloric intake of 2500 calories sufficient for men 65 years of age and over, and 1700 in women in the same age group. Fifty per cent of the men and forty-seven per cent of the women are more than ten percent above their optimal weight, and the excess of caloric intake replaces muscle tissue by fat. Such an accumulation of fat affects the organism unfavorably, and leads many times to a disturbance of the circulation and gastrointestinal activity, with a decrease in longevity. *Stare* recommends, for elderly people, a relatively high intake in proteins, meat, eggs and milk in order to maintain nitrogen equilibrium. Where aged persons cannot afford such a diet financially, a mixture of cereal products to which amino acids, such as lysine, are added are to be preferred. Lack of sufficient proteins in the diet can cause hypoproteinemia with the symptoms of senile pruritus, bedsores, wounds that do not heal and chronic eczematous dermatoses, which we find so frequently in senile patients. Moreover, the phenomena of fatigue, edema, anemia, and lowered resistance to infections in many old people might be related to a low protein intake. Therefore old people should reduce their caloric intake, especially in regard to fat, and take instead more proteins.

According to *McCay* (85), mechanization has decreased human movement so that the typical older person can live with very little compulsory exercise. Hence, his intake of foods, in terms of energy, usually will amount to only 1500 to 2000 calories, or about half the intake of an adult or a large youth. With this lowered intake of food, every effort must be made to insure high quality, in terms of essentials, because the need for such elements as calcium does not decline in proportion to the need for energy. In fact, the requirement for calcium rises in old age and may exceed the amount needed at any other period of life. Likewise, the need for vitamins and proteins seems just as high in old age as in middle life.

The second great hazard in later life is the temptation to consume foods that provide little besides energy. The two that create the greatest danger are alcohol and sugar. The next two, in order of importance, are cooking fats and white flour. With the exception of alcohol, these substances all offer the additional temptation of being cheap sources of energy. They are not cheap, if they lead to years of ill health in later life.

The old person, more than any other, needs to shop for natural foods, that are both economical and rich in essentials. Some of these foods are dry skim milk, soy flour, dry brewer's yeast, wheat germ, potatoes and whole wheat flour. The best meals are those rich in vitamins, such as heart, kidneys and liver. Eggs are nearly complete and the current fear of them, because of their cholesterol content, is not justified.

Since the older person may be dependent upon foods ready to eat, he should give special attention to basic products, such as bread. Bread can be made from excellent formulas containing milk, wheat germ, soy flour and yeast, or it can be made very poorly of white flour with few additions. What is true for bread is also true for breakfast cereals and sweet baked goods.

The older person can help his own diet by mixing dry skim milk or dry yeast into his foods. He can keep a sugar bowl on his table filled with powdered bone meal, and another filled with yeast or wheat germ. These supplements can be eaten at each meal. Milk is probably the best food for later life. Tests with animals have indicated, that they can be reared and kept for the whole of life upon no other food than fresh milk. Older, as well as younger, people can profit by the use of more milk.

Among the plant proteins, the best is that from soy beans. This can be purchased as flour and used in many foods.

Brewer's yeast is one of the richest natural sources of both protein and water soluble vitamins. It can be taken suspended in water just before meals by those who tend to become overweight. It can be used to lessen the need for insulin by diabetics. It may help prevent constipation; but it may cause trouble for those afflicted with gout since it is rich in purines.

Nutrition during later life requires regular study by every individual to insure sound food habits, and to avoid the pitfalls of alcohol, sugar and fat.

The neurological aspects of aging have been described by *O'Leary* (91). This author believes that the norms for neurological evaluation of aging subjects differ from those for average adults, in several respects. As aging progresses, the individual becomes less adept at fine movements. Habitude may be characterized by semiflexion at the principal joints, resistance to passive movements and slowness of willed activities, giving the impression that significant involvement of the basal ganglia exists. However, a general outfall of neurones may lead, in age, to a predominance of the flexor musculature, and the infirmities of joints and tendons also contribute to the change in posture. The same musculo-skeletal infirmities may contribute to the shortening of stride and unsteady gait which lead eventually to a shuffling, propulsive wide-based walk. The musculature may be hypertonic and the knee jerk overactive during normal aging; ankle jerks may be much reduced, but are rarely absent unless that finding has clinical significance. Again, vibratory sensibility is often diminished so significantly in the distal parts of the extremities (particularly the legs) of old people, that this test loses some of its value in detecting evidence of posterior column involvement, such as occurs in combined sclerosis. When it is only reduced or perverted (as, for example, being experienced as hot or cold) in the very old, the observation has debatable significance. Small pupils and slowness of pupillary response, amounting to sluggishness, may be due to atrophic change in the iridial musculature.

Certain neurological symptoms are encountered, commonly enough, in aging patients. Among these are syncopal attacks and vertigo. Less frequent, and usually associated with significant organic cerebral pathology, are senile tremor, Parkinson syndrome, chorea and convulsions.

Wexberg (114) made a comparison of neuropsychiatric conditions in American Negroes and whites, and came to the conclusion, that there are three cerebral conditions in which there is a definite difference, as to racial incidence, between Negroes and whites. Cerebral syphilis is by far more frequent among whites than among Negroes. The same holds true for senile dementia and for Parkinson's Disease, but not for cerebral arteriosclerosis. Not only the racial factor, but nonspecific exogenous factors ought to be considered, to explain the lower incidence of certain cerebral diseases in Negroes as compared to whites. It is a general experience, among populations of the same racial extraction, that, for instance, general paralysis is more frequent among highly civilized groups than among primitive ones—thus, the southern Negro seems to be comparatively protected. The same seems to be true for senile dementia. It is not a question, whether the Negro brain is less susceptible to senile processes, but it is a question of how the total personality of a particular social and cultural type stands up, under the wear and tear of civilization.

Whereas a nonspecific exogenous (cultural and social) factor appears to be responsible for the difference of incidence between Negroes and whites as far as senile dementia is concerned, the same does not hold in arteriosclerotic disease of the brain, which is not so much a disease of the brain, as a disease of the blood vessels.

Hauser and *Shanas* (46) studied trends of the aging population in the U.S.A. by comparison of fertility and mortality rates. These authors concluded, that in the

United States declining fertility and mortality have operated historically to produce an aging population. Until the passage of restrictive immigration laws in the 1920's, the tendency toward aging was retarded by the influx of large numbers of immigrants. With the decline in immigration and the changes in birth and death rates, which have occurred since the 1920's, the population of the United States has aged more rapidly than ever before.

Death rates in the United States have been declining for at least as long as any records are available. The data for the period before 1900 are fragmentary. In 1850, however, expectation of life at birth, a summary measure of the death rate at all ages was 38.3 years for white males in Massachusetts. By 1900, the Massachusetts male expectation of life at birth had increased to 44.3 years and by 1940 to 63.3 years. By 1948, life expectancy for white males in the United States had increased to 65.5 years.

The relatively small gains since 1900 in the expectation of life of those at the higher ages focus attention on the next frontier in the conquest of disease—chronic and degenerative conditions. One third of all deaths in 1900 were attributable to pneumonia, influenza and tuberculosis, diseases of the younger and middle years. By 1948, these three infectious diseases accounted for less than 7 per cent of all deaths. The leading causes of death in 1948 were diseases of older persons—heart diseases accounting for almost one-third of all deaths, cancer accounting for one-seventh, and then cerebral hemorrhage and nephritis.

The rapidly increasing number of older persons at the present time and in prospect, is, in the main, attributable to the increasing number of births in the United States in the latter part of the last and the early part of the present century. Thus, the increase in number of persons 65 and over from about 3 million in 1900 to over 12 and $\frac{1}{4}$ million in 1950, primarily reflects the increase in the annual number of births from 1835 to 1885.

As a measure of the increasing importance of the problems of aging in the decades which lie ahead, it should be noted that the number of persons 65 and over will increase to between about 17 and 20 million in the United States in 1975. The decrease in number of births in the late 1920's and early 1930's, however, will produce a temporary decline in the number of older persons between 1986 and 1998—a decline of perhaps 25 percent.

Despite such variations as reflect the cyclical variations of the birth rate, the long time trend will nevertheless, for many decades to come, result in an increasing number and proportion of older people in the United States.

Generally, it can be said, that old age does not involve the brain exclusively or even predominantly, but the whole organism as to substrate and function. It appears doubtful that genetic, metabolic, and morphogenic changes alone are able to explain the whole process of aging. *Malamud* (84) is of the opinion that aging, as a phenomenon, cannot be solely restricted to the brain and central nervous system, but that other organs of the body become involved, and attributes as much importance to social and psychological factors in the process of aging, as he does to the biological aspect. For example, anxiety and tension may psychosomatically influence brain circulation. Personally, I am inclined to give the problem of anxiety, which can cause cerebral spasms, a greater role than has been done in the past. Numerous case histories reveal that the geriatric patient who suffers an emotional shock, may, in consequence, succumb to cerebral spasms with headache, dizziness and fainting spells, followed by temporary paralysis of his extremities. Abnormal reflexes, which last for a few hours, indicate disturbances of the pyramidal tract. However, rest and papaverine medication can make it possible to overcome the paralysis, in many instances, in less than six hours. This treatment suggests that the relationship between tension, anxiety, and emotional stress to the origin of cerebral spasms, should not be overlooked. We all know that emotional stress, causing hyperacidity and disturbance of the circulation in the mucosa of the stomach, might be conducive to peptic ulcers with all their typical symptoms. In a similar way, frequent cerebral spasms, caused by tension and anxiety following an emotional stress, might also cause definitive damage to the metabolism of the brain, and to the brain cells themselves, and cause symptoms, dependent on the area involved. It is well known that essential hypertension is a consequence of a psychosomatic factor, and does involve, with preference, compulsive personalities who have worked hard all their lives and are overly strict, rigid and conscientious in their work. They do not enjoy recreation or relaxation of any kind or are too busy to give this time and thought.

English and *Weiss* (113), *Grinker* (42) and others have found the psychosomatic background of essential hypertension to be related to suppressed hate feelings against authority figures. That general arteriosclerosis, and cerebral arteriosclerosis might, at times, follow such essential hypertension, causing cerebro-vascular accidents, can easily be understood. Cerebro-vascular accidents represent, with the exception of coronary thrombosis, the greatest cause of mortality in the United States at the present time. Therefore, I believe that certain sociological and psychological factors can cause tension and anxiety, which, in turn, eventually produce physiological changes in the brain and in the central nervous system. These correlated factors are of more importance than recognized in the past.

THE SOCIOLOGICAL ASPECT

THE sociological aspect of aging is connected, I believe, to a high degree with three important problems. First, voluntary or involuntary retirement; second, our cultural attitudes toward elderly people; and, finally, the feeling of economic insecurity.

Badly managed retirement is, indeed, according to my own observation, the most frequent precipitating factor causing emotional upsets in elderly people, which often leads to hospitalization. When older persons do not have hobbies and interests developed in earlier years, which are able to occupy their time and thus their minds after retirement, they are unable to relax and to enjoy life. Too much inactivity makes them feel useless and superfluous, causes them to concentrate their interest on physical sicknesses, which can create many psychosomatic complaints and depressions. Retirement often causes a severe loss of self-esteem. To lose one's goal in life means for many old persons the end of all hopes and of life itself. Many old people have for years held their mind and their body together by compulsive work, and are not accustomed to relaxation, and, not knowing what recreation means, have in later life a complete breakdown of their physical and mental health. They can experience sudden and severe confusion and disorganization. They are really "lost" in the true and symbolic sense of the word (118).

28

Elderly persons must, therefore, have something to retire to. To find suitable hobbies and interests for them, to help them relax and be less anxious, to help them to "recreate" a new life, is, indeed, one of the most important goals of our preventive treatment for emotional disorders in aged persons.

Burgess (6, 7) and co-workers have made an extensive study of the occupational differences in attitudes toward aging and retirement at the Industrial Relations Center, University of Chicago. They come to the conclusion that there is a great difference in retirement planning between at least two occupational levels, the upper level occupational group and the manual worker. The supervisory-professional group shows a more favorable attitude toward old age and retirement planning. The manual worker reveals greater difficulties in the areas of mental outlook toward old age, financial planning, family and friends, meaning of work, retirement planning, social adjustment and job satisfaction. *Burgess* and his co-workers come to the conclusion, therefore, that retirement programs should be designed differently for these two occupational levels. The upper-level occupational groups need a greater opportunity to reinterpret and to assimilate their knowledge, while another program is needed for the manual worker, who frequently cannot find in the concept of retirement and old age a promise of a meaningful and well rounded life.

The same author has described, in a special study, the principal trends of personal adjustment in old age. According to *Burgess* (8), these include:

> Lower average years of schooling. This finding is in agreement with census data for the United States. It reflects the fact that each younger age group in our so-

ciety has had on the average more education than the preceding age group.

A higher percentage of widows and widowers. This trend emphasizes the increase, in number, with increasing age of persons bereaved by the loss of a spouse, who do not remarry. It is much greater for women than for men. In 1949 of all persons 65 and over, 24 per cent of the males and 54 per cent of the females were widowed.

A higher percentage living in dependent family relationships—in institutions, with sons or daughters, or with relatives.

A decrease in amount of close companionship. This is caused not only by the death of spouses but by the loss by death, change of residence, etc., of intimate friends.

A decrease in participation, as shown by attendance at meetings, offices held, number of hobbies, and plans for the future.

A decline in the gainful employment of males. Of all men 65 and over, in 1949, less than one-half (44 per cent) were gainfully employed.

Greater dependence on pensions, old-age assistance, and children for support. Of all persons, 65 years and older, in the United States in 1949, about one in four received social insurance and related benefits, and about one-fourth were on old-age assistance rolls.

Increase in physical handicaps, illness, nervousness, and a decrease in feeling of satisfaction and health.

Increase in religious activities and dependence upon religion. Frequency of church attendance drops in the eighties and nineties. Incapacity to go to church, however, is more than made up by listening to church services over the radio and by Bible reading.

Decrease in feelings of happiness, usefulness, zest, and a corresponding increase in lack of interest in life.

Lower median score, indicating poorer adjustment. Attitude scores are representative of the way older people react to their experiences in the major areas of their life, such as work, family, friends, recreation, leisure, and religion. They include, also, their statements of attitudes on health, economic security, zest for life and happiness.

Richardson (95), in a recent report on retirement by personal interview with 244 retired men in Scotland, tried to define in more detail the reasons why people retire, especially on medical grounds. He also made an investigation regarding the reemployment potential of these retired men and the use they have made of retirement. Over one-half of the group had a disability of occupational significance. The most common disabilities were heart disease, arthritis, and bronchitis. Retirement had been due most frequently to ill health or action by the employer, but the cause of retirement varied with age and social class. Half of the retired men had not found a contented way of life. In contrast, however, almost all those doing part-time work were satisfied with their compromise between full-time employment and complete retirement. The main activities of the retired men were helping at home, walking and gardening. The prevalence of true hobbies was low.

White (115), in an interesting article on the problems of retirement, points out that to anyone, who feels that his work is useful to society, retirement is repugnant. To anyone who finds activity necessary to health, retirement presents a critical problem in rearrangement. To a factory worker who has been tied to a machine for most of his life, retirement may seem the long-awaited release from bondage. To a creative person, retirement seems physically impossible, even if it were to prove financially feasible. To those who are emotionally unequipped to face the facts of old age, retirement is frightening—a symbol of approaching death. To anyone who feels that making money is the most fun there is, retirement sounds dull and empty. To anyone who has always gone somewhere in the morning, even to a

place he has not particularly liked, retirement seems like
the removal of the most steadying thing of all, his destina-
tion. To the person whose family cares and responsibilities
have increased with the years, whose dependents have mul-
tiplied, retirement—and the reduction of income—seems
utterly bewildering. To the person who has become emotionally attached to an organization, retirement seems like
compulsory divorce from a beloved spouse, an act of in-
credible cruelty. To a great many millions of workaday
toilers in the American vineyard, who keep their health
and do their jobs, retirement comes like a slap in the face;
it carries the implication that their powers have waned,
their day is done, their countenance is no longer a welcome
sight around the shop. Since there are almost as many problems of retirement as there are people who work for a living, it is no wonder that the subject is much in the people's
minds in this age of industry, in this land of extreme busy-
ness, where the very thought of anyone's dropping out of
the parade is disturbing if not degrading.

Shock (104) has given much thought to the problem of
old age and retirement. He concludes that, to keep old
people in emotional health, flexible plans for retirement
have to be worked out. The status of the person's physical
health remains an important factor determining employment, but emotional factors too, have to be given much
more consideration. This author advocates a plan of gradual retirement over a period of years, whereby the older
worker would be able to develop other interests or hobbies
outside his job. In this way a better adjustment to the
status of retirement can be achieved. It seems that in the
age group of 65 and over, more women than men remain
employed, and that women in the higher age group usually
outlive men.

Donahue (21), using statistical material, came to the conclusion that the middle-aged population, that is people between 45 and 64 years of age, will climb from 34 million in 1955 to 43 million by 1975 and to at least 53 million by the year 2000. The same author assumes that, in 1975, our older population in the U.S.A. will have approximately 12 million women and 9 million men. It is a fact that many old people over 65, belonging to both sexes, are still competent and able to do most work efficiently. Compulsory retirement at 65 or beyond is not the solution of the problem. Therefore, job counseling services for older workers and community programs to help them to retain their social usefulness are recommended.

Streib and *Thompson* (109), in a recent research project at Cornell University, found that, in elderly persons, their concept of anticipatory retirement is of great importance. These authors suggest retirement should be considered as a process which goes on over a period of time and only ultimately may lead to a state of being "retired." Problems pertaining to adjustment precede retirement by a considerable period of time. These ideas are furthered by *Tibbitts* and *Jones* (56), who believe that we should consider the person's adjustment at the age of 50, or even earlier. We then would be able to assess more precisely the individual's capabilities to adjust to retirement.

Giberson (33), in a valuable paper, points out that for the industrial worker, retirement looms ahead of him as a dread thing, the end of his importance to himself and to his company. He fears the incompleteness which his remaining years promise him. He is utterly unprepared for leisure. He is inarticulate about this, of course. His fears may come out in cantankerousness and officiousness, and he may try the patience of a whole organization before he retires.

This author recommends a gradual retirement plan

which would acclimate the worker to his new leisures and new horizons because of the medical dangers of sudden retirement—the nonadaptation to new routine, the lethal cessation of physical activity. Mentally, too, there is the danger of an aggravated irritation, of childish and unsocial petulance, that may transform a fine citizen into a liability. These dangers can be avoided by an active program, set in motion years before retirement. The worker's imagination could be kindled by the possibilities of the leisure opened up for him upon retirement. Leisure clubs might be organized, for instance, where all the colorful details of fishing, gardening, or useful social activities are emphasized and made available.

A good program should include some concrete evidence of the esteem and respect in which the older employee is held. In the interests of general morale, and in the efficient use of its resources of skill and judgment, industry itself should arrange some means of keeping in direct contact with its retired employees. Such precautions as these are not impractical; they are merely prudent savings of morale and skill. While the elderly worker might exhibit some loss in coordination and in physical endurance, these are frequently compensated by a gain in judgment and in working skill. Slight adjustments in working conditions and in speed rates are apt to make him even more efficient than younger workers, concludes *Giberson*.

If the elderly industrial worker is reluctant to change his ways, his reluctance stems mostly from caution. The older employee is apt to be settled in routine with orderly habits. These have created the only world he knows, and he has invested a lifetime in that world. Any sudden change threatens his world and his investment. Most of his trouble on this score is caused by his inability to make a transition from older to newer conditions. Perhaps a transition can be engineered for him, or at least his own made easier. He is haunted by the threat of exclusion, and he feels a discrimination where none exists. He is no longer rich in time and energy, and his knowledge of his own limits sets him apart from younger employees as effectively as his gray hair. He is cautious about new things because he has so little energy to spend; when a new road opens up, he knows that he can go only part of the way, and that he may not be around long enough to see any fruit from his efforts. He is apt to feel left behind and unconsidered; such a feeling can, in extreme cases, develop into sickness. The sequence leads to the feelings of being unwanted, barely tolerated, to suspicion of ordinary motives, fancied cruelty and to paranoid retaliation. Furthermore, the industrial elderly worker is jealous of his dignity. When a man works for years, making objects that disappear as soon as made, he has nothing tangible left to indicate his expenditure of energy; his only remaining gage of success or failure is the attitude shown toward him by his superiors and his fellow workmen. Respect shown him is proof that he has not been a failure. He is quite often deeply bored and unconscious of that fact. He has a hunger for significance, but the symbols about him do not add up into something personally important. Though he would deny this vehemently, his job and his home have become worn and threadbare. He needs a change of pace and an autumn tonic. He has a dread of insecurity, both in the economic sense and in the sense of dependence upon warm human contacts. These feelings are usually accompanied by a rankling sense of unfairness. He is as good as he ever was, yet should he be insubordinate and lose his present job, he would be unable to secure another one. He feels caught in a trap with, possibly, unprotected and meager old age ahead. Retirement, even on pension, will destroy his present life and offer no comparable life in exchange.

These observations of *Giberson* about the older worker are very impressive. They appear in no such clarity to the worker himself, but, allowing for individual variability, they can be traced as the starting point for many psychiatric cases.

Senator Desmond (18) describes the best rule to follow for retirement, and recommends that retirement has to be: fitted to the individual's needs, activity must not cease, and it must be conceived not as a "drawing back," but rather as a new turn in life's road, filled with new challenges, new opportunities. Synthesizing the findings of science with the personal experiences of the successfully retired, there are, according to *Senator Desmond*, five basic principles for making retirement a golden era of satisfaction and happiness:

1. Start planning the non-fiscal aspects of retirement when you initiate your fiscal program for retirement. Begin in your 30s and 40s to work on your plan.
2. Don't stop working abruptly; slow down gradually.
3. Make useful activity the core of your retirement plans.
4. Develop now an interest outside your business or profession that you can ride as a hobby, when you retire.
5. Devote part of your retirement to civic or charitable service.

Successful retirement is one of the most difficult achievements of a lifetime, as hard as the climb to the top in business or finance or law. It requires careful thought. Too many persons begin in their 30s and 40s to invest in annuities or to build up investments for retirement, but neglect, until the day they retire, planning what they are going to do with their retirement years. Everybody should allow himself at least 10 years, if possible, to develop and test his plan.

Frank (27), discussing sociological problems in connection with age, stresses the importance of the fact that we are in process of changing from a large dependent kind of population to a large dependent aged population. Statistics indicate, however, that there will be no diminution, but a probable increase in the number of people in early and middle adult life constituting the working population; therefore, this increase in dependent aged persons does not mean a reduction in the employable working population. The more serious question is, according to *Frank,* whether or not we can find a way of using this working group to meet the need for a larger total national income, to take care of the dependent aged. A large group of aged persons in our population will have votes and might become a formidable pressure group for pensions of all kinds. The employment of older people encounters some difficulties, because of technological changes and the slowness with which the various service activities are being organized. The modern trend in industrial techniques and processes does work against the older worker and, in many factories, the decreasing need of skill on automatic machinery, with technical control, likewise depreciates the experience of the older worker. *Frank* thinks that, due to changes in the age distribution of our population, the need for a social, industrial, professional and political reform has to be considered, a reform of far-reaching magnitude and significance, few of which we have scarcely begun to recognize, let alone to study.

Presently, a few investigators are giving great importance

to the problem of modern housing in regard to the well-being of our elderly folks (59, 60). Since the beginning of the twentieth century, there has been a tendency to leave rural districts and move to the city. There, many consider the chances of finding employment greater. Many find greater comfort in the fact that shopping centers are within easy reach, and entertainment and recreation are more readily available. Broadly speaking, there is a growing tendency to industrialization. The household has broken down into components of one-generation and two-generation family units, because these smaller groups are more adaptable to an urban-industrial, mobile society. If so, there may be a better possibility of finding work in factories. As a consequence, houses and farms in rural districts are abandoned. Small apartments for workers in the city are more desired. This factor again gives rise to many new problems, especially for the elderly. Lack of space in city apartments, which are relatively more expensive than farm or rural housing, brings about overcrowding in small apartments where, many times, three generations have to live together. The old person then may have to live with his children and grandchildren, rarely has a separate room and is unable to find enough peace and rest. He or she may become a "shut-in"; and, when the urgency for room space increases as more children arrive, he may consider himself, and be considered in turn, a burden. In recent years some special housing facilities have been created with the help of local communities, state or federal governments, where old people can live, peacefully and undisturbed, with relative comfort and little expense. However, the question arises if these special housing projects for elderly are an ideal solution. Perhaps, staying in the community with their own family and in relatively close contact with the younger generations should be preferred. Does old age represent a group which should be isolated and live by itself? Should old folks have their own recreation, diets, attitudes, special comforts, and their own ideas about people and life, or should they better be part of the whole community, and especially their own families? There are as many arguments in favor of such special housing projects as there are against them.

The same problem arises in psychiatric hospitals. Should there be special geriatric wards, or should geriatric patients be mingled with younger adult patients of different age groups? Is continuous contact with younger people necessary and desirable, or do younger persons pose an emotional threat to the older generation?

After many years of close observation and study of this specific problem, the author (122) came to the conclusion that from the standpoint of administration, separate geriatric units in psychiatric or general hospitals provide greater ease of patient management. The author feels that, in general, the aged patient can benefit more from this milieu than he can from mixing with younger adults on the ward. In similar ways as children's units, psychiatric or otherwise, have their definitely individual traits and attitudes, so geriatric units, too, have definite features of their own. Activities including industrial, occupational, and recreational therapy have unique methods geared to operate within the limitations of the aged patient.

Linden (76) has described the rationale for such a psychogeriatric care and developed an outstanding geriatric treatment and research center in Norristown, Pa. He outlined the following suitable program:

A program for the care and treatment of the emotionally ill aged and the building structure, in which it will operate, must be oriented to all their needs. While their requirements are essentially threefold, sociologic, physiologic and psychologic, they are manifested in physical activity. Among the senile aged this usually follows an almost universally characteristic sequence of events:

1. Cultural rejection.
2. Self-rejection.
3. Anxiety and panic.
4. Psychophysiologic exhaustion.
5. Psycho-sexual regression.
6. Withdrawal of object interest (isolation).
7. Restitutive phenomena with enhancement of pathologic mechanisms.
8. Autistic and dereistic preoccupation.

While physiologic decrements and true organic deterioration are largely irreversible, the psychologic factors are amenable to appropriate therapy in a well integrated setting. It is even probable that physiologic aging can be halted to some degree as mental attitudes are favorably affected.

Each of the above enumerated stages in the development of psychopathologic senility requires its own specific counteractant. In its simplest form, however, a program of treatment must contain these three elements:

ACTIVITY—as the bulwark against stagnation and regression.

RESOCIALIZATION—to combat isolation and effect a return of cultural values.

PSYCHOTHERAPY—to diminish the urgency of pathologic defenses and reactivate wholesome functioning.

Practice has already demonstrated that a thorough program brings about substantial results and should contain most or all of these items:

1. Congenial housing:
   a. Discreet privacy.
   b. Opportunities for socialization.
   c. Esthetically pleasant surroundings.
   d. Weather-oriented buildings.
   e. A maximum of convenience.
      1) Short distances to facilities.
      2) No necessity for climbing.
      3) Extra toilets, washrooms and drinking stands.
      4) Bedside furniture.
2. Activity:
   a. Work periods.
   b. Play periods.
   c. Privileges as rewards and treatment.
   d. Continuous scheduled functions.
3. Group formations:
   a. Recreation.
   b. Psychotherapy.
   c. Occupational therapy.
   d. Entertainment.
   e. Religious services.
4. Emphasis on personal appearance:
   a. Personal hygiene routines.
   b. Availability of colorful and fashionable clothing.
   c. Beauty parlor or barber shop.
5. Emphasis on personal dignity:
   a. Privacy.
   b. Appropriate freedoms.
   c. Attention to individual needs.
   d. Adequate staff of indoctrinated nursing personnel.
   e. Private laundry and ironing facilities.
   f. Some opportunity for dietary menu selection.
   g. Opportunities and facilities for snack feeding.

6. Facilities for physical health:
   a. Treatment area—away from residential wards.
   b. Continuous health surveys.
   c. Available consultants and special services.
   d. Energetic treatment of physiologic needs.
   e. Appropriate nutrition and supplementation.
   f. Enlightened nursing personnel.
7. Specific psychiatric therapies:
   a. Individual psychotherapy.
   b. Group psychotherapy.
8. General psychotherapies:
   a. Indoctrinated personnel.
   b. Avoidance of "mothering."
   c. Building atmosphere of optimism and hopefulness.
9. Community contact:
   a. Radio and television.
   b. Periodicals and books.
   c. Voluntary community visitation program.
   d. Visits by families and friends.
   e. Adult education program.
10. Welfare and follow-up:
    a. Staff action for outside placement.
    b. Social service department.
    c. Informative literature on departure.
    d. Legal and financial assistance.
    e. Availability of clinical services.

According to my own clinical experience at the Geriatric Treatment and Research Unit at Osawatomie State Hospital (Kansas),* even modern drug therapy for geriatric patients calls for special attention in regard to allergies and toxic effects. The methods of technique in psychotherapy

---

* See the *Menninger Quarterly*, Dec. 1958, pages 13-21.

are much different than the ones with younger adults. However, elderly people should never be completely isolated. Frequent visits with younger adults, especially with children, are necessary and desirable and should be encouraged. All three generations give to each other something of great importance. The life experience—the patience, greater sympathy, wisdom and understanding—of very many old folks should be utilized by the less mature and still growing generations to their own benefit and progress.

To have children and grandchildren near is not only an aid to overcome old people's loneliness, but it very often symbolizes older people's goal in life. In their relations with grandchildren or children, parents and grandparents are frequently reminded of their youth. They feel themselves reborn in their children and would like to help them in many ways. They try to educate, to advise, to protect, to lead, and find in these duties a fulfillment of their own life. Youngsters help them to play, to relax, not to take things so seriously, to laugh again, to remain young in spirit and to understand the problems of the younger generation. Older people indeed become less rigid, less stiff and seclusive, and appear happier, when contact with younger persons is maintained. However, the playfulness of the youngster must not become a burden and a stress. Children and grandchildren should realize that older people frequently like to be alone; tire more easily; need more sleep and rest, occasionally even in the daytime; and, they do not wish to be burdened with too great responsibilities for others any longer. At times, older people like the quietness of meditation and thought, often to prepare themselves for the life after death. Being aware that life may soon end for them, they need time to accept this idea and must struggle to overcome their fear. Only when they have worked through these feelings and are free from resentment and regret are they able to continue to live happily. When elderly persons see, however, hostile competition from the younger generation, who want the oldsters out of the way as quickly as possible, then the relationship between the older and the younger generation becomes disturbed, and hate is engendered. Therefore, tact on both sides will be necessary. Younger people should respect the older people's feelings and try to understand their handicaps, their sicknesses, their inability to be playful, to take certain responsibilities and to plan a life in the future.

On the other hand, youngsters should be prepared to accept from the older generation what they alone can give them—the fruits of a life experience, patience in reaching out for an individual's goal in life, making careful and consistent plans, work and relaxation, thoughts about how not to lose themselves in unnecessary, superfluous and harmful vices, and striving to recognize the true values of life, how to obtain and hold real friendships, to make matrimony and family life more harmonious and rich of fulfillment and to accept the individual's own handicaps and shortcomings without complaints and resentments. Only at a higher degree of maturity, which comes with age, can we realize that wrong done to others in our lives has only harmed ourselves and, being free from many unconscious strivings of our "ID,"* hate subsides, and love toward others grows and develops. Especially, when our sexual drive and erotic feelings toward the other sex become less urgent as in older age, can many stress situations in life be avoided, and our energy then becomes free for

* ID: In Freudian theory, that part of the personality structure which harbors the unconscious instinctive desires and strivings of the individuals. See "A Psychiatric Glossary" by the Committee on Public Information, American Psychiatric Association, 1957.

many hidden and undeveloped creative powers. There-fore, old age can have certain definite advantages younger people are unable to obtain.

Another important fact, which I would like to point out on this occasion, is the advantage of having a mixed group of both sexes in such a geriatric unit living together. The author (121) observed that many geriatric patients, re-leased from hospitalization after twenty or more years, have great difficulty adjusting on the outside in nursing homes, foster-homes, or in their own families because of previous lack of contact with persons of the opposite sex. Women remain scared of men and men of women, when they have not conversed together for many years, when they have never had picnics, dances or other relaxation together. Even sitting at the same table with persons of the opposite sex becomes a problem, after many years of isolation. Erotic feelings, suppressed or repressed for a long period of time, without outlet of any kind, might break through and induce the patients to become upset, disturbed and may even be responsible for a relapse into a psychotic state. Life in a hospital has to be as natural as possible and sub-stitute, to a certain degree, for home life. Rooms with plenty of space, air, sunshine, nice curtains on the windows, attractive pictures on the wall and with the mingling of elderly persons of both sexes in the dining room, during occupational and recreational activities and especially in group psychotherapy (119) has definitely great therapeutic value. Geriatric patients, as the author could prove, not only adjust more easily and better, when the sexes are mingled in a psychiatric hospital, but for them the step of leaving the hospital and starting a new life in a non-hos-pital environment, is less stressful, with fewer relapses into their sickness, and therefore fewer readmissions to the hos-pital.

Another factor of great importance for the better understanding of the sociological problems involved in old age
is our own cultural attitude toward the senior citizen. Our
century is the "century of the child and the youth." We
all are directed toward social and economic goals and are
driven by an irresistible force to achieve them. We live in a
world of continuous competition and, therefore, we have
to work compulsively and strenuously to be able to take
a place or to hold one. We live in continuous anxiety and
tension for one reason or another. We decide that "time is
money." We are overburdened with work, have no time for
recreation, for relaxation, and sometimes not even for
sleep. We lose the connection with Mother Nature and
with the rhythm of life. Music, art, literature, for us, are
considered a "waste of time." We find relaxation not even
in our family life, not even in love. Sexuality frequently
has taken the place of true love, and the responsibilities of
our family life make us worry day and night. We live without imagination, without play, without phantasy, without
romance. We sometimes lose the feeling of being human
beings and do things mechanically and without interest.
Then, as the end of our life comes nearer to us, we are
exhausted and have the feeling we have not really lived at
all. In such a world of tension, of compulsion, of work, and
of competition, elderly people are considered a burden.
They know it, they feel it, they see and hear it and are
unhappy and dejected. Elderly people cannot compete with
this modern trend, but they are unable to change it. We,
however, can and should do something about it (118, 122).
But this is a subject for more extensive study.

In this connection, I would like to say something about
a paper, "Relationship between social attitudes toward
aging and the delinquencies of youth." *Linden* (79) points
out the link between our lack of respect toward the elderly

person, our cultural attitude of rejection and intolerance, our feelings of impatience, hostility and annoyance with the elderly parents or grandparents, with the increase of juvenile delinquency. Children, who cannot identify with father or grandfather, who consider elderly parents useless and burdensome, who laugh about senior citizens, who grow up without parental support, and without ethical judgment, are frequently in a state of rebellion. Where life experience and wisdom are held in no esteem, where parents and grandparents are not an example of goodness and personal worthiness, where authority is rebelled against, because it is not considered, we create an atmosphere of freedom without limits, of wanting without boundaries and of egocentricity. When the child does not learn to look upon the elderly as an object of respect, then the door is open for rebellion and disobedience. Police control can never substitute for parental control. Punitive measures will never be as effective as the parents' love and understanding. Our own cultural attitude is therefore partially to blame for the increasing delinquency of our children, who do not learn, from us, the true values of life.

Dunham (23) points out that a cultural factor is involved in our attitude toward elderly persons. For instance, in China, where the utilitarian, individualistic personality type of the Western society is less prominent, and the cultural and institutional forms of ancient China are still preserved, at least partially, and the ancestor worship and the philosophy of Confucius are still taken into consideration, the male grandparents are without doubt the head of the family and worthy of respect, authority and even veneration. A good relationship between parents and children and cooperation and understanding between the generations represents one of the most important features of Chinese religion, politics, welfare and economy. Security for older parents will always be provided, and the interests of the younger generations play a secondary role. The son or the sons have to cultivate the land for the parents, when they are unable to do so, and to have a son, for elderly parents, is the best insurance against the handicaps of old age. Public charity, therefore, is hardly known in China and would be considered shameful for old people. The same patriarchal attitude is characteristic of many Oriental races. In India as well as in Israel, the same philosophy and attitude is preponderant at the present time as in past centuries. In China rarely do elderly persons feel rejected and dejected, as in our modern European or American civilization; they are, on the contrary, happy, serene and show friendly benevolence and, frequently, physical charm and rarely suffer from resentment, bitterness and depression, so often seen in the facial expression of the oldster in the United States. As for my own experiences for $9\frac{1}{2}$ years as a physician in China, there are fewer psychotic reactions to be found in patients suffering from the symptoms of chronic brain syndromes associated with cerebral arteriosclerosis or with senility. When the hour of the death comes near, death is greeted with serenity and accepted as a preparation for a better life afterwards. Chinese and Indian people believe in paradise or "Nirvana," and life, for them, is only a preparation for this.

The third factor to consider is the feeling of economic insecurity from which so many old folks suffer. Old people have to live protected from physical and emotional sickness and from the most urgent needs of our daily life. Public welfare helps, we know, when the need arises, but this help should be given willingly and effectively, so as not to cause an emotional blow and severe loss of self-esteem. Special housing projects, hospitals for the chronically sick, rehabilitation and recreation centers have to be built. Such a program, however, asks for understanding of the problems involved, and should be of the greatest concern to our legislatures. Money appropriations for Day Centers for old people are wisely spent, and the successes obtained by outstanding Day Centers as the Sirovich and the Hodson Day Centers in New York or the Senior Citizen Center in San Francisco speak for themselves. In these Day Centers, elderly people meet during the day and remain under the supervision of a trained social or recreation worker. They work, play, talk together and enjoy doing carpenter work, paintings, drawings; they sing in a choir, play theatre, write poetry, read books, study languages, do their own laundry, their own cooking and eventually have their own administration. These Senior Citizens learn to enjoy life again. They feel the security only a home and good company can give, and remain emotionally healthy by feeling needed and wanted. They stay intellectually alert and forget their misgivings against a society and a world, which does not reject them any more because of their old age. They build friendships and learn to trust people and do not feel old, because their ability to achieve is restored. Low self-esteem, depression and hostile feeling against members of their own family and their neighbors are overcome, and enthusiasm and optimism prevail. Therefore, these Day Centers are one of the most important steps in the prevention of mental sickness and emotional trouble in old age (60).

Levine (72), in an interesting paper, describes the need for recreation centers for the aged. This author points out that the Day Center can be a substitute for the loss of the work day; can be instrumental in prolonging the period of usefulness; it can extend the feeling of acceptance and belonging in the older person, and it can give meaning to the latter part of life by developing a dynamic program for the older person.

It is generally accepted, that each individual ages at his own speed or pace; and, in the same individual, different functions age at different rates. It is, therefore, the "content" age, rather than the birthday or chronological age, that becomes important in working with older people. In these Day Centers medical findings should be utilized, to help the older person to a realization of the remaining strength available to him, and to plan for its utilization. We also should be aware that people have many areas of competency that a busy work life has not permitted to develop. It is to be hoped, through a testing process, to uncover these areas and combine those areas of competency with the strength remaining to the individual.

According to *Levine* the Day Center program should have for its objectives:

1. The promoting of the social and emotional adjustment of the older person through activity.
2. To make possible for the older person the maximum use of the capacities least impaired and of capacities least used.
3. To cut the period of illness from a matter of years to a matter of months.

Only in this way can we prevent many emotional and physical sicknesses of elderly persons. The accent should, however, never be on welfare but on rehabilitation. Most elderly persons can still do useful and meaningful work, if they find the right understanding for their problems. They might work more slowly and finish a task not as fast as a young person, but they might be able to work with great exactness. In Switzerland, for instance, many watch-makers are old people because of their greater experience and patience. In the U.S.A., to a limited degree, we are using the skill of elderly persons as furmakers, tailors and even as machinists. In politics, in art, in philosophy, in science, I would like to remind you of the achievements of Churchill, of Ghandi, of Toscanini, of Einstein, of Albert Schweitzer, who, in spite of their old age, have been able to create things all humanity is very proud of. We do not need to take a pessimistic attitude in regard to elderly persons. They do not have to regress, to deteriorate, to become useless, and be considered superfluous. They can offer something younger persons do not possess—wisdom, patience and life experience—which should and can be utilized for the benefit of all. Therefore, the emotional health of our old folks should be one of our communities' most important concerns and interests. The problem of emotional sickness of the elderly can never be resolved by our state hospitals, state institutions, nursing homes, private clinics, or medical practitioners. It is not enough to send old people to state institutions for treatment, even if we had enough psychiatrists, competent in handling this kind of patient. When we return our patients from state institutions to the same stress situation, to the same cultural attitude of rejection, we let them feel unwanted and a burden in the circle of their own family or community. When we do not help them feel economically secure, without humiliating them, and do not improve our retirement system and put it on a more individualized base, our treatments in state institutions, private clinics and in medical practice generally will be of temporary benefit only, unable to prevent relapses of emotional disturbances in old folks. It is about time, because of the ever growing number of old people in our modern world, that we become aware of its immense social and political importance, and that we do something constructive about it.

We definitely need a kind of guide to social action as developed at the 11th Annual Conference on Aging on June 25, 1958, in Ann Arbor, Michigan, where the following concepts are derived from the presentations made in that conference and which have been selected, because they are pertinent to many fields of action:

1. Individual differences continue to be important in the middle and later years. Hence, older people cannot be considered as if they were all alike in physical capacity, psychological functioning, health, job efficiency, etc.

2. Aging is not a disease. There are, however, physiological deficits which accompany growing older and which must be considered in the development of services and program.

3. Social and psychological growth may occur concurrently with biological decline.

4. Patterns of personality organization and response tend to be stabilized by middle age. They are susceptible to change, but radical alterations in personality patterns should not be expected.

5. The basic needs of older people are the same as the basic needs of all people. Resources for satisfying them, however, tend to be diminished in later life.

6. Individual and group behavior is influenced by environmental as well as physical factors.

7. Older people vary widely in what they consider the "good life." Their definitions reflect not only individual differences but cultural and social backgrounds.

8. At the present time, certain cultural values in the

social environment of the U.S. adversely affect older people. Examples of such values are accent on youth and the importance of work in fixing status.

9. Cultural values change. We are now in a period of transition. With accumulated experience, adequate social action, and education, the status of older people can change.

10. Potentiality of older people can be developed in many directions, if there is effective freedom of choice and opportunity to pursue it.

THE PSYCHOLOGICAL ASPECT

THE emotional needs of the elderly people have been described lately by a number of outstanding physicians and psychiatrists. It has been stated that the cause of many of the mental breakdowns in later life can be found in experiences dating from childhood and adolescence. We know that these early experiences play an important part in the origin of schizophrenia and manic-depressive psychosis. Now we recognize that mental disturbances like involutional psychosis and senile dementia also have their roots in childhood experiences.

In a well known paper, published in 1948, *Gitelson* (36) has given importance to the emotional aspect of aging. This author attributes six different patterns of adjustment in old age:

1. A decreased memory for recent events—a turning away from the painfulness of the present.
2. A sharpening of memory for the past, especially for time when life was successful.
3. A more self-assertive attitude as compensation for insecurity.
4. A mild depression caused by isolation and the feeling of loneliness.
5. Introversion and increased sensitivity with querulous and paranoid attitudes.

6. A free floating anxiety caused by death among the same age group, especially when relatives are involved.

The irritability of older psychotics often has its source in the inability to cope with the environment as well as in physical decline. Apathy, in elderly persons, can be considered as an outcome of the detachment of the individual from painful memories and events of his life. *Kaplan* (62) states that one of the effects of losing friends and relatives is to give the older person not only a feeling of being alone in the world but also a feeling that, without social ties, he is unprotected and insecure. Of a somewhat different opinion is *Overholzer* (92), who suggests that our attitude of over-protection of our old people results in personality change, and that we should be careful not to accelerate, in older people, their entrance into a condition of dependent helplessness. Loss of independent activity frequently produces an emotional crisis. Retirement for instance gives more opportunity for introspection, for self-evaluation, for the development of delusional ideas and for regrets. Older men, who tend to be more seclusive and withdrawn than older women, are more inclined to cerebral arteriosclerosis, while women suffer more from senile dementia.

The problem of becoming aware of being old has been studied by *Jones* (55, 56) and others. Subjects have been asked, how and when they noticed for the first time they were growing old. *Jones* found that, in most cases, the following symptoms were mentioned by his patients:

1. Breakdown of the locomotor apparatus.
2. Difficulties of a nervous kind.
3. Sense—organ impairment.
4. Deterioration of the skin and the hair.
5. Increased tendency to fatigue.

6. Greater need for short periods of sleep interposed during the day.

Kuhlen (68) points out that the biological changes accompanying old age have been extensively studied in themselves, but have not yet received the attention they deserve from the point of view in which they are perceived by the individual. Such changes imply much more psychologically than a diminution of actual functional capacity only. Greying hair or increased girth can become quite threatening and losses in strength, sensory acuity, sexual capacity and energy level may represent losses in ability to achieve gratifications in accustomed ways. Special threats to the aging person appear to be developments which reduce mobility and restrict the individual's freedom to make constructive adjustments to frustrating situations: lack of advancement in position, increased responsibilities to a growing family, and biases against employment of older individuals. According to *Havighurst* (47, 48) an adequate Ego function is not only dependent upon freedom from physical disease or crippling, but also involves the element of hope. Everyone will be able to endure pain and hardships if there is hope that the suffering eventually will come to an end and the future will be brighter. The child gives up many of his gratifications for responsible achievement, because each step brings approval and love from his parents. Indeed, approval and love from others and the individual's yearning for them is an important factor in a healthy Ego function. Hope for a better future, love and approval from others often is lacking for old folks and their life is empty because of lack of interest of friends, neighbors and relatives. Therefore, it is extremely difficult for them to maintain a good emotional equilibrium.

It is well known that paranoid trends become more evident in senile persons, especially if their personality traits have always been of a suspicious kind. Old people often feel unwanted, and this realization may be conducive to delusional ideas. Frequently, the content of the delusions centers around the idea of being robbed, of being poverty stricken, or of being poisoned. The tendency to commit suicide increases with the higher age group. The loss of loved ones, or physical sickness with a poor prognosis, may precipitate this tendency and always must be given careful consideration. Criminal offenses generally decrease with old age, but sexual offenses, fraud, violation of the narcotic laws, arson and poisoning frequently bring older people to court and, afterwards, to mental institutions.

Studies of the emotional needs of the elderly have been made by comparing their attitude with the attitude of the child (78). The child has been found to be a fundamentally dependent person getting acquainted with independence, which appears desirable but full of danger. The child makes progressive efforts toward mastery of his helplessness. The aged person, on the other hand, has gone through this state of independence, but his self-sufficiency has become seriously threatened by decreasing effectiveness and by the progressive breakdown of his defenses. The child emerges from isolation and helplessness and renounces his private strivings to please society, or the family. The older person likes to participate in everything belonging to society, but society shows a hostile and rejecting attitude towards him. The child has unlimited energy, great ambition and psychic elasticity which helps to keep him from being hurt, and he reaches out for the future. The aged person finds his supply of energy diminishing. He fears the future, is blind to reality, and finds himself in a continuous state of disillusionment. He no longer believes in a world of love and peace, and loses interest in accomplishment.

Meerloo (88) describes one of the first symptoms of the elderly emotional disturbed patient as the spontaneous return of emotions repressed in childhood, giving evidence of a breakdown of mental defenses. In several types of climacteric neurosis an increased ID drive and increased aggression become evident. The climacteric or postclimacteric woman, for instance, frigid before her menopause, now tries to attain sexual satisfaction, liberated from responsibility and fear of childbirth. She is hastening for complete gratification before she dies, showing a phobic acting out of what has been repressed for many years. In my experience, such behavior causes anxiety neuroses of a severe degree, and often leads to divorce and domestic problems. Especially when the conscience is strong, the anxiety does increase accordingly and gives evidence of a severe internal conflict. Furthermore, with diminishing Ego control in advanced age, aggressive impulses might break through leading to self destruction or to destruction of family relationships.

Often these drives become more evident and less controlled by the use of alcohol or drugs. Increased sensitivity to environmental influences is observed. Change in environment, retirement from business, lowered income, forced moving, and replacement by younger people with loss of prestige, might percipitate a mental disturbance. The aged person cannot accept the reality of being mortal, and in his dreams secret plans for immortality play an important role. The fear of insomnia, according to *Meerloo,* represents the dread of loneliness and death. Some old people bury themselves in squalor and refuse any contact with the outside world; others hoard money and possessions and live continuously in fear of losing them. Old age might therefore be considered a traumatic neurosis with continuing trauma.

With the increasing emphasis on body function and "anal"* hoarding, the elderly person grows more and more narcissistic and stingy. For the geriatric patient, the diminishing of his heart function means symbolically loss of love and should be well understood as a psychosomatic reaction.

Goldfarb (37, 38), in his long experience with psychotherapy of geriatric patients, describes that many of these patients appear to be outwardly depressed but are more self-aggrandizing than self-depreciating. Although feelings of failure and frustration are expressed, the environment is usually blamed and attacked, frequently in a paranoid fashion. These patients reveal little evidence of guilt, but fear of retaliation is usually present. They do not seriously contemplate or attempt suicide although they may make such gestures. Although they often express a wish to die, to go soon, or to have it over with, they protest lack of courage, or give moral and social reasons for their self restraint from suicide. Outstanding is the complaint of joylessness, lack of pleasure, feelings of futility and hopelessness. For them, eating, sleeping, personal relations, work, hobbies and entertainments are not pleasurably anticipated, presently enjoyed or happily reviewed. Therefore *Goldfarb* believes that, in geriatric patients, the absence of true depression is related to a decreased capacity for affectionate relationships. They fear most of all the loss of the material implications of personal relationships: personal care, protection and dominance over those from whom they derive care. They are unable to retain the friendship of persons who can afford protection, and are concerned about desertion and abandonment. The joylessness, their

---

* *Anal erotism:* Pleasurable part of the experience of anal function. In later life anal erotism usually appears in disguised and sublimated forms. See: *A Psychiatric Glossary by the Committee of Public Information,* American Psychiatric Association, 1957.

sense of futility and hopelessness is a means of obtaining and guaranteeing care. Old folks want pity, compassion and care from parental surrogates, and frequently do not permit themselves pleasure. They often prefer to feel persecuted and deprived. At times such a facade of helplessness and hopelessness masks a persistent attitude of hopeful expectancy.

Gerty (32) considers, that the appearance of many mental breakdowns during the aging period may be caused by a collapse of the personality under stress and emphasizes as etiologic factors, conditions other than organic disease. Some of these personality disorders are due to a continuation from the preinvolutional period, and represent psychotic regressions and manic depressive and schizophrenic reactions. Others show psychoneurotic regressive tendencies. The same author believes that the pathological condition producing a picture of mental symptomatology in old people may not be primarily in the brain. Even aphasia may result from impaired brain circulation, resulting from a combination of cardiac disease and narrowed cerebral vessels. Organic factors, involving the whole organism and not the brain alone, and emotional factors taking into consideration the premorbid personality and the individual reaction to a stress situation, appear to be of greatest importance.

Masserman (86) points out that, in regard to the dynamics of aging, it is important to differentiate between the actual disabilities of aging—that is: the diminished capacity to perceive, differentiate, abstract and evaluate the environment, and respond in a properly versatile and efficient fashion—as well as the reaction of the individual to such impairments. The essential dynamics of the aged depend on the attempts of the individual to compensate for his declined powers and status. Similarly as the paranoid grandiosity of the paretic is not caused by the disease itself, the aged tries strenuously to reassure himself of his physical competence from bedroom to golf course. He builds and defends philosophic and mystic systems promising some form of immortality. Finally he tries desperately, and sometimes pathetically, to retain or reestablish what human relationships he can salvage here on earth.

Busse (10, 11) is of the opinion that guilt is apparently an unimportant dynamic force in the psychic functioning of so called normal elderly persons and is seldom conducive to depressive features, so frequently seen in geriatric patients. According to *Busse* the older person is no longer living in a highly competitive situation, which mobilizes hostility and aggressive impulses which end in self condemnation. This lack of competition with others, however, appears to foster the development of inferiority feelings which form the basis for depressive episodes. The aged person cannot counteract inferiority feelings by demonstrating his superiority through competition. The source of the inferiority feelings are primarily an inability to fulfill needs and drives and the doubts, which develop, when the oldster is reminded of the decreasing efficiency of his bodily functions. Therefore biological, sociological and psychological alterations have to be taken into consideration in relation to the origin of depressions in geriatric patients.

Schiele (98) stresses the importance of decline in strength and the loss of physical attractiveness of old people. Social and economic limitations and infirmities impose handicaps on the older age group. The loss of good looks or physical prowess represents frequently a severe blow to self esteem. In addition to these defects, reduced visceral function, diminution in the various senses (particularly of sight and hearing), reduced sexual function, failing memory and increased lability of emotions become a reality. These are enough reasons why an elderly person might feel restless, unhappy, unwanted and rejected. Low reserves and loss of flexibility make the elderly person more vulnerable to physical and psychological stress. As he cannot deal effectively either with the future or the present, he tends to overvalue the past. This is one of the reasons why neurotic complaints among the aged are common. However, the type of disorders that occur depends largely on the personality organization.

The old age adjustments are similar to those of childhood and youth, and old age fears and anxieties are likely to be reactivations from childhood. As *Cicero* insightfully mentioned centuries ago, "Those with simple desires and good dispositions find old age easy to take, and those who do not show wisdom and virtue in their youth are prone to attribute to old age those infirmities which are actually produced by former irregularities."

The great lack of flexibility indeed is one of the older person's greatest problems and causes much anxiety especially in regard to adjustments or readjustments in a new environment or in a new neighborhood.

Dunbar (22) is of the opinion, that a healthy senescence depends on the maintenance of homeostasis, which *Cannon* (13) described as the capacity of the living organism to maintain a stable equilibrium, or as the tendency, when subjected to shock, to restore its pre-existing equilibrium. The concept of homeostasis depends, however, according to *Selye* (101) on the "General Adaptation Syndrome" which occurs as defense against stress with triphasic periods of "Alarm," "Resistance," and "Exhaustion." The physiological response to a stress situation might follow a normal pattern, but it might be conducive to a pattern suggestive of a neurosis or psychosis. Therefore, it is necessary for the

the physician to evaluate the nature and intensity of the stress for each individual in case of sickness. It appears that the greatest stress situation is due to frustration and failure, acute illness, catastrophe, marriage and problems concerned with fertility and sterility, divorce and death.

Very old people (one hundred years or older) in relatively good health have been examined in regard to those stress situations in an experimental setting (22). The results reveal, that persons, who live to be very old, have been able to avoid frustrations and to escape conflicts with authority. They ascribe special value to independence and attempted to apply the principles of democracy as a basis for cooperative and productive living. They worked hard and long hours, but were not anxious to get to the top, and therefore did not suffer from hypertension. They have a social character, a sense of humor and are well liked. They do not worry about things beyond their control, and are disinclined to argue. They try to avoid tension, daily annoyances, and frustrations that produce chronic stress, leading to homeostatic disequilibrium. They are honest with themselves and face sickness and frustrations squarely and objectively without fear, and therefore remain more healthy, and succumb less to acute sicknesses. They are able to stand catastrophe in their family life and do not react too severely to personal injury. They are not easily "shocked."

Liebman (75) gives importance to the fact that marriage does not present a special problem for "potential centenarians." They enjoy marriage, have a low record for divorce, have relatively many children, and eventually marry again in their nineties if the spouse dies. The problem of fertility cannot force them into a stress situation. Death does not arouse fear and desperation in them, but is considered as a natural consequence of life itself. Religion for them is important and helps them to overcome their fear of death. Hobbies, interest in recreational activities, and friendly interpersonal relationships are used to avoid the feeling of being lonesome and isolated. The "potential centenarian" is rarely in a hurry, and dislikes working under pressure. In his casual, quiet way he is able to work long hours without feeling rushed, and therefore, he does not suffer easily from circulatory damage. He is able to interrupt his work for a brief rest, a walk, or for recreational activities. Abuse of drugs, coffee or alcohol is avoided. The "potential centenarian" is seldom to be considered an "accident prone" person, seeking relief from tension and anger by impulsive actions and unconscious suicidal attempts. He is able to think before he acts, and therefore he is in less danger of getting hurt emotionally.

Only by maintenance of physical and emotional homeostasis have many artistic, literary and scientific achievements been made possible at advanced age. Michelangelo completed the dome of St. Peter's at 70, Sophocles wrote *Oedipus Tyrannus* at 80, Goethe, past 80, completed *Faust*, Gladstone became Prime Minister at 84 and Handel, Hayden and Verdi created immortal melodies after the age of 70. Creative powers, genial ideas and artistic greatness are not bound to any age, but seem mainly to be an affair of will-power, workability, endurance, enthusiasm and homeostasis.

Cosin (14, 15) who had much experience in screening and treating confused and regressed geriatric patients at Oxford, states that in the progressive intellectual deterioration and decreased ability to adjust in the elderly, many factors are involved. These include cerebral anoxia due to organic disease: cerebral vascular incidents, trauma, hypotension during anesthesia, postoperative surgical shock, malnutrition due to insufficient intake of protein, iron and vitamin B, and especially chronic anxiety states due to emotional problems in connection with the family. This author stresses the fact that the intellectual deterioration of the elderly can be prevented by a suitable handling of his environment, by Day Hospital treatment, and especially by individually applied occupational therapy.

Grotjahn (43), who has treated geriatric patients successfully with psychoanalysis, believes that growing old is often felt as narcissistic trauma, for it represents and repeats a castration threat. The neuroses of old age are defenses against castration anxiety. Old infantile wishes do not die; nor do they fade away; they are waiting to return. There are three different potential reactions for the elderly to the existential problem of aging. The first is the normal solution: it aims at the integration and acceptance of a life, as it has been lived. Then there is increased conservatism and rigidity of the Ego, trying to hold the line of defenses according to the pattern of previous neurotic adjustment. The third possibility is frank neurotic or frequently psychotic regression.

The successes obtained by *Grotjahn, Meerloo* and others in treating elderly patients by psychoanalysis changed the pessimistic attitude of psychiatrists regarding the treatment of the aged considerably. This new optimistic orientation toward geriatric psychiatry represents a great step forward. It appears that psychotherapy with elderly patients is facilitated by the fact that resistance against unpleasant insight is frequently lessened in old age. Acceptance of the idea of growing old and its meaning, and the dealing with the problem of dying, appears to be the central problem of psychotherapy with geriatric patients, depending very much upon the therapist's personal attitude and philosophical conviction.

The author was able by means of sodium amytal interviews to confirm *Grotjahn's* idea, that extreme restlessness in geriatric patients and symbolic castration fear are connected. Death, for these patients, appears to be the final castration.

Kaufman (64) discussing the analytic treatment of depressions in old age, describes the inverted Oedipus complex occurring in such instances. Aged and dependent individuals may regard adult offspring much as they formerly regarded their own parents. Considerable ambivalence takes place when the patient, who once helped his child in growing up and was the authority figure, now has to take orders from his children.

The same author has made important studies on the psychoanalytic viewpoint of aging and comes to the conclusion that, according to psychoanalysis, the personality structure and its subsequent development is genetically predetermined. The solutions and adjustments arrived at in childhood will determine the behavior of the individual at crucial periods in his life. Relatively little work has been done by the psychoanalysts with the middle-aged or older group. *Freud* (30), in one of his earliest papers, discussing the application of psychoanalytic technique as a therapeutic measure, states: "Near and above the fifties, the elasticity of the mental processes, on which the treatment depends is, as a rule, lacking. Old people are no longer educable, and, on the other hand, the mass of material to be dealt with would prolong the duration of the treatment indefinitely." In 1898, he stated that "psychoanalysis loses its effectiveness after the patient is too advanced in years" (29). These statements, of course, influenced Freud's followers a great deal, and, therefore, therapeutic work was not attempted until many years later, when *Abraham* (1) tentatively and cautiously presented some clinical observations on several patients over fifty. According to *Abraham* the prognosis is more favorable, if the neurosis is in its full severity, after a long period has elapsed since puberty, and after the patient has enjoyed, for at least several years, a sexual attitude approaching the normal. *Abraham* demonstrated that the personality of the individual was not quite as rigid, for the purposes of psychoanalysis, as one had been led to believe, and that the psychoanalytic method was applicable. The findings, he reported, in themselves did not throw much light upon the specific problem relating to old age and aging. Later on *Jelliffe* (53) and his coworkers tried psychoanalytic therapy with older patients. *Jelliffe* reported psychoanalytic studies with two patients well advanced in years. According to these experiments the psychoanalytic technique, with relatively little modification, was applicable, partly as a therapeutic method and definitely as a research instrument. Another important psychoanalyst, who devoted an entire chapter of her book on the sexual life of women to observations on the climacterium, is *Deutsch* (19). This author points out the importance of puberty and its interrelationship with late life. The period of puberty represents a return of many sexual feelings with a reaching out for new love objects.

According to *Deutsch* puberty is accompanied, on the psychological side, by definite endocrine changes leading to increased sexuality. The shadow of the climacterium is, however, already present at this period. The woman, even after a successful adjustment, already begins to feel uncomfortable about her age and begins to deny it quite soon, in anticipation of that period of life, when she will no longer be able to function as a child-bearing biological unit. The climacterium is psychologically a traumatic experience to every woman. It marks the end of her femininity. Menopause comes as a narcissistic injury. With the onset of this period, which goes hand-in-hand with a regression in physiological functioning, there may be a heightening, perhaps as compensation, of libido activity. There is a displaced reaching out for new love objects. The woman who, up to now, had perhaps been well-adjusted, begins to try to act "young again." She may become dissatisfied with her husband and even attempt flirtations or affairs with younger men. This period can readily be recognized as the so-called "dangerous age." There begins a phase of "retrogression," a regression to abandoned infantile libidinal drives. The genitals become depreciated as an organ. Inaugurated by a biological signal, just as in puberty, there is an effort at first to retain libido,* then there may be a reproduction in all the essential details of the puberty conflicts. According to *Deutsch*, "it is now too late." There are two climacteric phases, both repetitions of the phases of puberty in reversed order. In the first phase of attempted compensation, the libido is strongly directed towards the object, with a strong narcissistic longing to be loved. In the second phase there is a devaluation of the genital, renewed masturbation of the clitoris, turning away from reality, and reversed Oedipus phantasies.

The function of reproduction and the loss of direct object relationships are the center of conflict in the aging woman. During the corresponding age period in the male, the focus of conflict also centers around the sexual problem. The principal difference, however, between males and females in old age, is in the field of sublimations. Some observations show that the intensity of aggression, which the reactionary old man displays towards youth, depends in part on how revolutionary his own attitude has been during puberty.

* *Libido:* The psychic drive or energy usually associated with the sexual instinct. See: *A Psychiatric Glossary by the Committee on Public Information*, A.P.A., 1957.

The type of psychotic manifestation one meets with during this period of life, gives an indication of the conflict situations. The frequency of agitated depressions, so-called involutional melancholia, and various paranoid conditions is indicative of the regression which takes place. In many instances in women there is a renewal of bisexuality with a tendency to masculinization.

With advancing age, however, certain pathologic factors, too, become important: organic changes in the central nervous system and especially in the brain substance itself, causing the features of the organic brain syndrome.

Quite a few psychoanalysts have made important studies on these conditions and came to the conclusion, that psychotherapy can be of definitive value even in cases of organic brain damage.

In relation to general paresis, *Ferenczi* and *Hollos* (26) and *Wallerstein* (111) have shown that certain psychological manifestations may be understood psychoanalytically and be treated accordingly. Other interesting experiments were reported by *Schilder* (99). To a patient, suffering from senile dementia, a frankly obscene story has been told. Then the patient was asked to reproduce it. In the reproduction the content of the story was changed by the patient to a more decent one: where the words "erect penis" occurred in the original story, they were replaced by the word "cigarette." In another instance symbolism, which occurs in dreams of a normal individual, was used. The importance of these observations is, that, even though part of the personality functions have been destroyed by organic disease, other psychological processes are retained. Indeed, it is quite possible that a study of just this type of clinical picture may throw a good deal of light upon the mechanisms of repression, symbolization, displacement, and other mechanisms, which play an important role in mental functioning.

Although there has been relatively little direct psychoanalytic experimental work or clinical observation of the type of psychological reaction, one meets with in organic brain disease, *Kaufman* believes that, although organic defect as such is definitely based on destruction of the central nervous tissue and is characteristic to varying degrees of all diseases of the brain, whether arteriosclerosis or brain tumor, the content of the forgetting may have definite individual psychological significance.

One important aspect of the problem of maturity is the question of the rigidity of the Ego. With increasing age the majority of people tend to become fixed in their opinions and reactions; as *Freud* has expressed it, they lack elasticity. The youthful radical matures into the older conservative. This is due, partially, to a more objective evaluation of reality factors with increasing age, but childhood conflicts appear to be present and are of overwhelming importance dynamically even in old age. According to studies of *Kaufman* and others, the neuroses and psychoses of this period are definitely of a pregenital type, for example the involutional melancholia with regression to orality. Instead of the anxieties dying out or being dissipated with the period of the climacterium, they actually become more threatening, and, in the face of "actual" conflicts, which cannot be solved, the individual regresses more to psychotic reactions. According to statistics, emotional disturbances appearing for the first time in later life, are more likely due to psychosis than to neurosis.

Other interesting observations with geriatric patients have been made by *Schilder* (100). This author believes that the apprehensions and fears of the presenium and early senium are overcome by deterioration. These patients may feel happy and strong again, revive heterosexual wishes, or may at least feel gratified by oral satisfaction. The fear of being poor, of being robbed or of being persecuted may persist, and may act as a constant stimulus to escape into a state of greater happiness. The aging and the senile may even try to get renewed satisfaction in the sexual approach to younger people. However, in the majority of cases, this approach to youth will remain in the realm of day-dreaming, phantasy and confabulation. There are indications that these regressions follow the pathways through which the individual has gone in childhood, adolescence and adult life. There are psychic compensations in senility. When the individual is no longer capable of enriching, or maintaining his relations to the outward world, he regresses to infantile situations and looks from there to new possibilities. The geriatric patient has a definite relation to time and space, though the objective facts of time and space are distorted. Even when the senile regresses, he does it differently than the schizophrenic. He cannot go back to a magic world, but remains in a world which fulfills the strivings and desires of his adolescence and manhood.

Bowman (2), in an excellent paper, described how physical changes affect emotions and intellect. Loss of hair, grey hair, wrinkles and other physical evidence of aging may be conducive to a feeling of inferiority. Decrease of sexual capacity and inability to enjoy sexual experiences, may be an important factor causing depressions. Such individuals might indulge in sexual phantasies, suffer from deep anxieties, and eventually commit suicide. On the other hand, elderly persons might consider the decrease of sexual drive as relief and freedom from something very disturbing and upsetting.

In regard to intellectual decline in elderly persons, *Bow-*

man describes the correlation existing between the physical and mental condition of the patient. Memories seem to get progressively worse from about 30 years onward, caused eventually by atrophy of the brain. However, memory loss can be partially caused also by loss of interest, and lessened intensity of feeling in the old person. Learning ability decreases with age, because learning of new things requires breaking down of long-established patterns, a difficult procedure for elderly individuals. Older persons sometimes feel, as their life span grows short, that there is no need for new experiences, and therefore they do not try to learn. Reasoning ability and perception of spatial relations decline with advancing age. Elderly persons can hardly deal with unfamiliar material. Imagination, judgment and wisdom might be affected to a variable degree. While many older persons have good judgment and reveal wisdom in their actions and are therefore welcome in councils of government and on the bench, others show considerable decrease of their intellectual functions and are unsuitable for such positions.

Ebaugh (24) stresses the factor of fear in old age. The old person is plagued by fear of physical infirmity, loss of economical security, approaching death, indifference of children, loss of friends and social contacts, loss of capacity of sexual gratification, and, above all, by the fear of useless loneliness. Frequently the family of aging persons reacts to these fears with resentment: they are afraid of restriction to their own freedom, of caring for an invalid, who can easily become a neurotic tyrant and can hardly control their own resentment against the elderly. The family increases the problems of the old person and eventually disrupts family life. Oldsters might also touch off anxiety in others, because hidden fears of sickness, death and disintegration are lurking in everyone. In this way even greater rejection of the unstable adult takes place.

Gumpert (44), in an interesting paper on "Geriatrics and Social Work," states that emotions often become highly sensitized in later years, and the emotional response seems to be stimulated by the process of aging. Our emotional structure, indeed, does not age or at least does so very slowly. Abnormal irritability, stubbornness or sullen resignation are often found in old folks, alternating sometimes without obvious motivation. Elderly people are emotionally unstable, breaking into tears or laughter on slight provocation. They can be frightened and suspicious and may be inclined to acts of violence or suicide. They may be stingy and become hoarders by collecting all kinds of worthless material, from which they refuse to part. Their sense of veracity is, sometimes, impaired, inducing them to use lies or phantasies as substitutes for lost memory or as a disguise for their inadequacy. Carelessness of appearance, untidiness and deterioration of manners are not uncommon. At times they reveal senseless obstinacy, while others can be too easily influenced and moulded. They can be exploited because of their loneliness and desire for affection, and occasionally might become prey for fakers or criminals. Furthermore, the aged brain may show signs of fatigue.

In my own clinical experience, periods of very active intellectual attention are followed by such signs of emotional fatigue, as confusion, lack of orientation, poor organization in discussion, tendency to talk too much, or to change the subject frequently. Emotional blocking with retardation of thought, movement and emotions might become evident, when the brain is exhausted, a fact, due perhaps to inadequate oxygen supply of the brain. A period of rest, after a time of intellectual fatigue and continuous tension, is therefore not only indicated, but restores the brain again to normal functioning.

We have to be aware of the fact that an emotional attitude might be connected with physical disease. Old folks with digestive disturbances, especially those suffering from a peptic ulcer, might be moody and occasionally bad tempered. Diabetic patients reveal a more or less evident emotional instability, due to continuous anxiety and fear of dying suddenly. Cardiac patients are generally known to be very restless, demanding and tense. Patients suffering from general and cerebral arteriosclerosis, when consciously or unconsciously aware of their handicaps, might become deeply depressed. Elderly persons might not only suffer from one, but from several physical handicaps and can be in a continuous state of anxiety and tension, due to the realization of their physical sickness. Prostate troubles are often the cause of elderly men feeling invalided and rejected. It is a fact that an old person can hardly be in perfect health; sickness, however, even chronic sickness, does not need to be considered hopeless and impossible of recovery.

Chronic sickness might stimulate the defense mechanisms of our body, developing a tolerance against pain and imbalance. Our potential faculties of repair and compensation are great and can be utilized for recovery. Sickness can be followed by convalescence, the most powerful force of regeneration in human life, and recuperation from sickness can be a great emotional experience by strengthening our failing powers of immunity and active self-defense. Our vital forces could be stimulated, and the accent should never be on custodial care but on rehabilitation. Even old people with serious chronic sickness can become useful and remain very active members of their profession and of society.

Physical handicaps might even become, by the mechanism of compensation, the cause and beginning of great creative powers, as has been proven many times. Everything depends on the individual's personality, on his emotional attitude to physical handicaps, on his optimism and his willpower. There is no reason, I am convinced, for elderly persons to react with the loss of their emotional equilibrium to some of the inevitable physical sicknesses associated with aging. Instead of revealing signs of intellectual decline and emotional regression, they can remain mature, self-reliant, independent, and feel happy and satisfied by reorientation of their goal in life and by stimulation of their creative powers. Aging should not evoke punitive, restrictive, uncompromising authority, but the elderly person can and should by his warmth, his humanism, his experience, his orientation around group principles be the leader of our community and, as *Linden* expresses it, "consultant in living."

I have observed that many geriatric patients have distinct ambivalent feelings toward life and death. They often want to die, believing they have nothing to live for. They wish for cessation of their physical and mental preoccupations, but, when they feel the hour may be near, become disturbed and afraid. They cling to others and want them near at all times. They especially fear the dark and request that the light be kept on all night. They may turn more toward religion, go to church often, confess and ask for their sins to be forgiven. Religion gives them emotional support and tends to relieve them from the fear that everything will soon come to an end.

Peck (94), in an interesting study on the *Psychological*

Developments in the Second Half of Life, states that old age brings to almost everyone a marked decline in resistance to illness and a decline in recuperative powers. This increasing experience with bodily aches and pains represents for many old folks a very grave insult. For people who have learned to define "happiness" and "comfort" more in terms of human relationships, of creative activities of a spiritual nature, their physical decline is of less importance, and mental and social powers might actually increase with age and compensate for the loss.

Chinese and Hindu philosophers as well as thinkers of the Western culture (Schopenhauer, Nietzsche and others) advocate a more constructive way of living in spite of the prospect of personal death. To live generously and unselfishly, to continue to build for a braver future through children, through contributions to the culture, through friendships are ways open for every human being and are, I think, the only understandable kind of self-perpetuation after death. Since death is an absolute certainty for everyone, real happiness, personal satisfactions, and contentment depend upon the capabilities of an elderly person to overcome his own clinging to a private, egocentric, separate identity in the interest of other individual's welfare and happiness. *Only he, who gives himself completely without regard for his own person, will at the end be free from anxiety and deep concern, when the last hour is approaching, and remain free and unhampered from emotional crisis in old age.*

Much has been written about the sexual problem in old age, and many studies have given this problem special consideration. *Hamilton* (45) expresses the opinion that sexual frustrations, so often observed in older persons, are related to somatic and environmental handicaps carried over from early life. Elderly individuals regress frequently to the

autoerotic and pregenital satisfactions of infancy. Masturbation and eroticism (the latter related eventually to in-
testinal difficulties), are common in the elderly age group.
The Ego strength diminishes, and the strivings of the ID
are suppressed with more difficulty.

Guilt feelings and a great deal of anxiety, in geriatric
patients, are due, in my observations, to these sexual strivings, condemned by both the individual and by the environment. Sexual strivings and excesses might become, in
old age, a source of physical sickness, because the associated excitement may contribute to circulatory disturbances
and their consequences. Generally, the erotic feelings of
elderly persons are directed toward younger persons, even
children, and may show themselves in attempted rape or
exhibitionism; more often, however, they are sublimated
and appear only in the form of normal, natural affection
of the aged for children and represent an effort to regain
their lost youth by identification.

Cameron (12), in an interesting chapter on "Neuroses
of Later Maturity," states that emotional disturbance in
later life is not due to signs of parenchymatous degeneration or to cerebral vascular disease, as it is often generally
believed, but attributes the emotional reactions of geriatric
patients to their status of being lonely, tired, loveless and
without hope. Conservatism and resistance to change,
whether of routine, arrangement, manners, morals or opinion, is characteristic of elderly persons. These tendencies
are not always symptomatic of repressed antisocial attitudes, but may be symptoms of physical decline.

To be uprooted by leaving their own country, city or
home, is one of the most important stresses for elderly
people, I believe, and creates, frequently, a great deal of
anxiety, depression and agitation. I have observed that this
resistance to every kind of change is one of the greatest

obstacles in having geriatric patients leave the hospital and always calls for special skill and effort.

Another meaningful factor for old folks is their resentment and bitterness in being replaced on their job and at home by the younger generation. Although many of them realize that this is in the nature of things and has to come sooner or later, they, nevertheless, do not like to sit on the sidelines, to be patronized or remain unnoticed.

Many elderly persons respond to this rejection with withdrawal, with a flight into phantasy, or with increased rigid and compulsive behavior. Their work or life attitude may become more and more orderly, regulated and schematic, in order to protect themselves against failures and mistakes. This compulsive orderliness is one of the first signs of decompensation, which the psychiatrist may detect, when he examines patients with a beginning chronic brain syndrome. It represents a mechanism of defense against emotional disorder and reveals itself, often, in psychological testing. Old people may start to simplify, to restrict their interests and their life, trying to eliminate the source of tension and anxiety, in the belief that they are no longer wanted or liked by others.

Malamud (84), in an excellent paper on the "Psychopathology of Aging," reports about studies of the personality organization in psychiatric disturbances of geriatric patients, and comes to the conclusion, that for overconscientious, rigid, and sensitive personalities, adjustment in later life becomes more difficult. The same author holds responsible for emotional disturbances in old age failure to provide old folks with special interests, to satisfy their needs in later years, sudden loss of beloved objects (husband, wife, children, the home, etc.), operations or injuries of organs generally related to reproduction (pelvic and breast operations, prostatectomies, etc.), and loss of social and economical security.

The intellectual changes in old people were studied especially by *Miles* (89) at Stanford University. He found that imagination seems to be ageless, and that verbal associations, interpretations of meaning, and recognition of relationships show less tendency to decline with age than do speed, organization, recall of unfamiliar material, and difficult logical procedures. The total intelligence quotient scores show a progressive decline with advancing age. *Wechsler* (112) points out that the curves show a parallelism between loss of brain weight and decline of ability with age.

Gilbert (34) has done well controlled studies about psychometry of the aged and aging and concludes that probably the best way of attacking the problem of mental decline with advancing years would be to follow through life a large number of individuals and subject them to various tests at intervals from childhood to senility. At present, however, this method is not suited to our needs, as we have no records of early mental tests of our older individuals and yet are faced with the practical problem of determining their maintenance or decline of mental ability. In spite of certain admitted inadequacies of our present tests, psychometry can even now render definite information on both the mental ability and the mental deterioration of older persons.

First, however, we must state definitely to what age groups we refer, when we speak of mental decline with advancing years. To plot a curve of mental decline, we must have norms at least for each decade of adult life. To measure groups of individuals between the ages of 40 and 70 covers too wide an age range. Our prime concern must be with individuals over the age of 60.

According to *Gilbert* there are two ways of measuring mental deterioration in the aged: 1) by the use of general intelligence tests, and 2) by the use of a test which will control the original intellectual level of the individual.

The use of general intelligence tests, to measure the mental ability of old people, has two faults: While speed plays an important part in the practical consideration of the efficient functioning of an individual, it does not tell us anything about his intellectual level, and often serves to obscure his real native ability. To measure general intelligence in adulthood, the tests should be standardized for each decade, for only thus can we compare the abilities of an older person with the general intelligence of his contemporaries.

The second important fault in the use of intelligence tests on older people is the failure to take into consideration the original intellectual level of the individual being tested. We may find that a group of old people scores at the average or below the average of a group of young people on certain tests, but this does not indicate whether or not any individual in this group has suffered a decline in mental ability. No numerical rating on a general intelligence test can tell us this, even if the test be standardized for each decade as mentioned above. For example, an individual, who scores above the average, may actually be deteriorated, in that he does so poorly compared with what he once could do. We must first know his original level of intellect before we can say he has or has not deteriorated mentally. The attempts to control this by means of educational and occupational levels are obviously unsatisfactory, because of the different opportunities, both educationally and vocationally, which have come with the passing years.

The Babcock Test of mental efficiency, a test first designed for the measurement of mental deterioration in psychotic persons, is an instrument which controls the original intellectual level of the individual. For this reason, this test is satisfactory for use with older people. This test is based on the assumption that deterioration occurs first in new learning and in the formation of new associations and last in earliest formed material. It does not mean deterioration of general intelligence but rather deterioration of one phase of intelligence—the efficiency phase which, after all, is the functioning side, which must interest us practically, if we are working with older people. The factor of speed has to be taken into consideration. Speed is, although not used to gauge the intellect of an individual, a factor of practical importance. For example, what good would it do for an individual to know the correct responses to make in driving an automobile, if in a crisis he could not make these responses quickly enough to avoid a collision?

The use of vocabulary as the control of original intellectual level will undoubtedly draw adverse comment, but investigators do agree that vocabulary shows marked resistance to age. Rather unexpectedly, it seems to depend relatively little upon the amount of formal education. For example, *Gilbert* found in persons in the sixties a number of individuals, who, without a day of formal schooling in their lives, scored higher on the vocabulary test than did some of his young college graduates. A good vocabulary seems to be a thing which natively superior persons acquire, regardless of educational advantages or the lack of them, and something which natively inferior persons cannot acquire, regardless of opportunity. On the other hand, vocabulary does not increase materially after school years. *Gilbert's* studies support this conclusion. Of special interest in this connection is the close similarity of vocabularies of parents and adult offspring, even when not living together. By this method then, we can make a true comparison of older and younger persons of matched intellect and also compare an individual's efficiency with that of his normal contemporaries of like intellect. This is a practical point to consider, particularly in connection with employment possibilities of older people.

Using this method, there is a definite decrease in efficiency for all levels of intellect in the sixties, the loss being greatest of tests involving learning and the formation of new associations, flexibility of perceiving relations, retention and motor ability and least on tests such as the giving of opposites, general information and simple repetitions. Taking the group as a whole, the per cent loss varies from 57 per cent loss in the learning of paired associates to 12 per cent loss in the giving of general information. The average loss is 29 per cent. Speed is an important factor on most of the tests, and when not weighted for time, the per cent loss of the older group decreases, but is still decidedly significant and remains greatest in the type of test which requires the formation of new associations and least in tests closer to simple vocabulary. There is a marked learning defect. There is very little overlapping in the efficiency indices of the older and younger groups, with evidence, also, of a progressive deterioration within the decade of life from 60 to 69 years inclusive. Another interesting point is a marked tendency for the very highest levels of intellect to show relatively less decrease of efficiency than those of lesser intellect, raising the question, whether it may not be that the greater the intellect with which one is endowed, the less he tends to deteriorate or the longer he tends to retain his original equipment of efficiency.

Individual differences in mental deterioration are great, and these are of practical importance to anyone working with older persons. Both physical condition and temperament are important considerations. Likewise, employment seems to keep up efficiency, although at times it is difficult to determine whether some of the unemployed are unemployed because they are inefficient or whether deterioration has progressed more rapidly because of the condition of unemployment.

Gilbert concludes that, although there are some in the sixties who are fit only for retirement or old age pensions, there are others who are capable of (and would be much happier) functioning at a decreased pace with remuneration scaled to output of work. There are others, particularly in the higher types of work, who are capable of producing at great value to society. It is not profitable to discard all aging individuals, regardless of individual ability or desire. We must not forget that the older person has fewer industrial accidents, spoils less material and causes less turnover than the younger person, thus to some extent offsetting his disadvantages of less speed and decreased adaptability. Also, the experience and knowledge he has gained in his own field with the passing years, are not to be lightly turned aside.

Granick (40) in a review regarding the psychology of aging comes to the conclusion that, in old people, the overall intelligence test performance shows a marked and progressive decline in relation to increase in age.

It appears that on subtests regarding vocabulary, general information and reasoning problems, in which speed is not a factor, older adults have an achievement comparable to younger subjects. Memory functioning, efficiency of performance and tasks involving the relinquishing of old habits, however, are found to be difficult for old people. Furthermore, projective tests reveal senescence to be associated with a decline in personality functioning in such important areas as flexibility and control, and social adaptability. Generally, however, the evidence would seem to indicate that old age does not mean, for the average person, increased emotional instability, despite the new problems of adjustment they encounter.

It is a fact also that people reaching old age become increasingly preoccupied with their health, material things and philosophic values. Religious ideas and feelings seem to become more personal and egocentric.

In these chapters, current biological, sociological and psychological concepts of aging have been reviewed. A vast amount of further information on this important and interesting subject will be forthcoming as more and more investigators become aware of the need in this field of medicine.

I would like to end with a few sentences of *Selye* (101) who wrote: "True age depends largely on wear and tear, on the speed of self-consumption; for life is essentially a process which gradually spends the given amount of 'adaptation energy' which we inherited from our parents. Vitality is like a special kind of bank account, which you can use up by withdrawals but cannot increase by deposits. Each exposure leaves a scar. Since we constantly go through periods of stress and rest during life, just a little deficiency of 'adaptation energy' every day adds up—to what we call aging."

REFERENCES

1. ABRAHAM, K.: *The Applicability of Psycho-analytic Treatment to Patients at an Advanced Age.* London, Hogarth Press, 1927.
2. BOWMAN, K. M.: Mental adjustment to physical changes with aging. *Geriatrics,* 2:139-145, 1956.
3. BUERGER, M.: *Altern und Krankheit,* 3rd edition. Leipzig, Thieme, 1957.
4. BUERGER, M.: Biomorphose oder Gerontologie? *Z. Altersforschg.,* 10:279-283, 1957.
5. BUERER, M.: Die Biomorphose des menschlichen Gehirns im Lichte seines wechselden Nukleinsaüre und Gangliosidgehalts. *Z. Altersforschg.,* 10:283-288, 1957.
6. BURGESS, E. W.: The older generation and the family in *The New Frontiers of Aging,* edited by Donahue, W. and Tibbitts, C. Ann Arbor, The University of Michigan Press, 1957.
7. BURGESS, E. W.: Round table meeting on psychiatric factors in aging, Annual Meeting, A.P.A. May 14, 1957, Chicago, Ill.
8. BURGESS, E. W.: Personal and social adjustment in old age, in *The Aged and Society,* Industrial Relations Research Association, edited by Milton Derber. Champaign, Twin City Printing Co., 1950.

9. Busse, E. W.: Mental health in advanced maturity, in *The New Frontiers of Aging,* edited by Donahue, W. and Tibbitts, C. Ann Arbor, The University of Michigan Press, 1957.

10. Busse, E. W.: The treatment of hypochondriasis. *Tri-State M. J., 2*:7-12, 1954.

11. Busse, E. W., Barness, R. H., Silverman, A. J. and Others: Factors which influence the psyche of elderly persons. *Am. J. Psychiat., 110*:897-903, 1954.

12. Cameron, M.: Neuroses of later maturity in *Mental Disorders in Later Life,* 2nd Edition, edited by Kaplan, O. S. Stanford, Stanford Univ. Press, 1956.

13. Cannon, W. B.: Aging of homeostatic mechanisms, in *Problems of Aging,* 2nd Edition, edited by E. V. Coudry. Baltimore, Williams & Wilkins, 1942.

14. Cosin, L. Z.: Current therapeutic and psychotherapeutic concepts for the geriatric patient, in *Progress in Psychotherapy,* edited by Masserman, J. H., and Moreno, J. L. New York, Grune & Stratton, 1957.

15. Cosin, L. Z.: The place of the day hospital in the geriatric unit. *Internat. J. Soc. Psychiatry, 1*:33, 1955.

16. Cosin, L. Z.: Discussion on geriatric problems in psychiatry. Proceedings of the Royal Society of Medicine, Section of Psychiatry, Nov. 8, 1955.

17. Cowdry, E. V.: Significant areas of research in aging. *J. Am. Geriatrics Soc., 3*:276-280, 1958.

18. Desmond, T. (Senator): You can't retire on your money alone, in *Young at any Age,* New York State Joint Legislative Committee on Problems of the Aging. Legislative Document No. 12, 1950.

19. Deutsch, H.: *The Psychology of Women,* vol. II. New York, Grune and Stratton, 1945.

20. Deutsch, H.: *Psychoanalyse der Weiblichen Sexual-*

funktionen. Vienna, Int. Psych. Verlag, 1925.

21. DONAHUE, W.: Emerging principles and concepts: A summary in Donahue, W. and Tibbitts, C., *The New Frontiers of Aging.* The University of Michigan Press, Ann Arbor, 1957.

22. DUNBAR, F.: Immunity to the afflictions of old age. *J. Am. Geriatrics Soc.,* 5:982-996, 1957.

23. DUNHAM, H. W.: Sociological aspects of mental disorders in later life, in *Mental Disorders in Later Life,* 2nd edition, edited by O. J. Kaplan, Stanford, Stanford University Press, 1956.

24. EBAUGH, F. G.: Age introduces stress into the family. *Geriatrics,* 2:146-150, 1956.

25. FENICHEL, O.: *The Psychoanalytic Theory of Neurosis.* New York, Norton, 1945.

26. FERENCZI und HOLLOS: Zur Psychoanalyse der paralytischen Geistesstoerung. *Beihefte zur Intern. Ztschr. Psychan.,* No. 5.

27. FRANK, L. K.: Discussion, in *Old Age and Aging. Am. J. of Orthopsychiat.,* 10:39-42, 1940.

28. FREEMAN, J. T.: The mechanisms of stress and the forces of senescence. *J. Am. Geriatrics Soc.,* 7:71-78, 1959.

29. FREUD, S.: Sexuality in the Etiology of the Neuroses. Coll. Papers, Vol. I. London, Hogarth Press, 1898, p. 245.

30. FREUD, S.: On Psychotherapy, Coll. Papers, vol. I. London, Hogarth Press, 1904, p. 258.

31. GERARD, R. W.: Some aspects of neural growth, regeneration and function. In *Genetic Neurology,* Chicago, Univ. of Chicago Press, 1950.

32. GERTY, F.: Importance of individualization of treatment in the aging period. *Geriatrics,* 12:123-129, 1957.

33. GIBERSON, L. G.: Industrial aspects of aging personnel, in *Mental Health in Later Maturity,* Federal Security Agency, United States Public Health Service, Supplement No. 168, pg. 22.

34. GILBERT, J. G.: Discussion in "Old Age and Aging." *Am. J. Orthopsychiat., 10*:59, January, 1940.

35. GILBERT, J. G.: *Understanding Old Age.* New York, Ronald, 1952.

36. GITELSON, M.: The emotional problems of elderly people. *Geriatrics, 3*:135-150, 1948.

37. GOLDFARB, A. I.: Psychiatric problems of old age. *New York State J. Med., 55*:494-500, 1955.

38. GOLDFARB, A. I., TURNER, H.: Psychotherapy of aged persons. *Am. J. Psychiat., 109*:916-921, 1953.

39. GOLDFARB, A. I.: Psychotherapy of aged persons. *Psychoanalyt. Rev., 42*:180-187, 1955.

40. GRANICK, S.: The psychology of senility. A Review. *J. Gerontology, 5*:44, 1950.

41. GRANICK, S.: Studies in psychopathology in later maturity, *ibid., 5*:361, 1950.

42. GRINKER, R. R., ROBBINS, F. P.: *Psychosomatic Case Book.* New York, Blakiston, 1953.

43. GROTJAHN, M.: Analytic psychotherapy with the elderly. *Psychoanalyt. Rev. 42*:419-427, 1955.

44. GUMPERT, M.: Geriatrics and social work. Conference presented at the Institute on Group Work and Recreation with the Aged. School of Applied Social Sciences, Western Reserve University, Cleveland, Ohio, April 16, 1953.

45. HAMILTON, G. V.: Changes in personality and psychosexual phenomena, in Cowdry (ed.). *Problems of Aging,* 2nd Edition. Baltimore, Williams & Wilkins, 1942.

46. HAUSER, P. M., SHANAS, E.: Trends in the aging population in Cowdry's *Problems of Aging,* 3rd Edition, edited by Lansing, A. I. Baltimore, Williams & Wilkins, 1952.

47. HAVIGHURST, R. J.: Personal and social adjustment in old age in *The New Frontiers of Aging,* edited by W. Donahue and G. Tibbitts. Ann Arbor, The University of Michigan Press, 1957.

48. HAVIGHURST, R. J.: Roles and status of old people, in Cowdry's *Problems of Aging,* 3rd Edition, edited by A. J. Lansing, Baltimore, Williams & Wilkins, 1952.

49. HEINRICH, A.: Beitraege zur Physiology des Alterns. *Z. Ges. Exper. Med., 96*:722-728, 1935.

50. HIMWICH, H. E.: Brain Metabolism and Cerebral Disorders. Baltimore, Williams & Wilkins, 1951.

51. HIMWICH, H. E. and HIMWICH, W. A.: Brain metabolism in relation to aging, in *The Neurologic and Psychiatric Aspects of the Disorders of Aging.* Baltimore, Williams & Wilkins, 1956.

52. HIMWICH, W. A. and HIMWICH, H. E.: Brain composition during the whole life span. *Geriatrics, 12*: 19-27, 1957.

53. JELLIFFE, S. E.: The old age factor in psychoanalytic therapy. *M. J. and Rec.,* January, 1925.

54. JONES, L. W.: Personality and age. *Nature, 136*:779-782, 1935.

55. JONES, H. E. and KAPLAN, O. S.: Psychological aspects of mental disorders in later life, in *Mental Disorders in Later Life,* 2nd Edition, edited by O. J. Kaplan. Stanford, Stanford Univ. Press, 1956.

56. JONES, H. E.: Notes on the study of mental abilities in maturity and later maturity, in *Research on*

Aging. Proceedings of a Conference, August, 1950, Univ. Calif. New York, Soc. Sci. Res. Council, 1950.

57. KALLMANN, F. J.: Heredity and aging, in *The Newsletter of the Gerontological Society. 4*:5, June, 1957.

58. KALLMANN, F. J.: The genetics of aging, in *The Neurologic and Psychiatric Aspects of the Disorders of Aging.* Baltimore, Williams & Wilkins, 1956.

59. KAPLAN, J.: Successful patterns of aging. Symposium presented at the Eleventh Annual Meeting of the Gerontological Society, Philadelphia, November 7, 1958.

60. KAPLAN, J. The day center and day care center. *Geriatrics, 12*:247-251, 1957.

61. KAPLAN, O. J., Editor: *Mental Disorders in Later Life,* 2nd edition. Stanford, Stanford Univ. Press, 1956.

62. KAPLAN, O. J.: *Studies in the Psychopathology of Later Life.* University of California Library, Berkeley, 1940.

63. KAUFMAN, M. R.: Old age and aging: the psychoanalytic point of view. *Am. J. Orthopsychiat., 10*: 73-79, 1940.

64. KAUFMAN, M. R.: Psychoanalysis in later life depressions. *Psychoanalyt. Quart., 6*:308-335, 1937.

65. KETY, S. S.: Human cerebral blood flow oxygen consumption as related to aging, in *The Neurologic and Psychiatric Aspects of the Disorders of Aging.* Baltimore, Williams & Wilkins, 1956.

66. KETY, S. S.: Circulation and metabolism of the human brain in health and disease. *Am. J. Med., 8*:205, 1950.

67. KOUNTZ, W. B.: Degeneration and regeneration, in

Cowdry's "Problems of Aging," 3rd Edition, edited by A. I. Lansing. Baltimore, Williams & Wilkins, 1952. p. 1061.

68. KUHLEN, R. G.: Age trends in adjustment during the adult years as reflected in happiness ratings. *Am. J. Psychol., 3*:307, 1948.

69. LANSING, A. I.; ROSENTHAL, T. B. and ALEX, M.: Calcium and elastin in human arteriosclerosis. *J. Gerontology, 5*:112-119, 1950.

70. LANSING, A. I.: Some physiological aspects of aging. *Physiol. Review, 31*:274-284, 1951.

71. LANSING, A. I.: General physiology, in *Cowdry's Problems of Aging*, 3rd Edition, edited by A. I. Lansing. Baltimore, Williams & Wilkins, 1952.

72. LEVINE, H. E.: State aid for recreation centers, in *Young at any Age*. New York State Joint Legislative Committee on Problems of the Aging, Legislative Document, No. 12. p. 144, 1950.

73. LEVINE, H. E.: Mental health and aging. Paper presented at the Annual Health and Welfare Council Meeting, New York City, N.Y., May, 1955.

74. LEWIS, W. H., JR.: Medicine and the aging population. The *J.A.M.A., 166*:1412-1419, 1948.

75. LIEBMAN, S.: Stress situations. Philadelphia and Montreal, Lippincott, 1955.

76. LINDEN, M. E.: Architecture for psychogeriatric installations, prepared for the therapy session on Geriatric Architecture of the Fifth Mental Hospital Institute, Little Rock, Arkansas, October 19-22, 1953.

77. LINDEN, M. E.: Effects of social attitudes on the mental health of the aging. *Geriatrics, 12*:109-114, 1957.

78. LINDEN, M. E.: Geriatrics, in *The Fields of Group*

Psychotherapy, edited by Slavson, S. R. New York Intern. University Press, 1956.

79. LINDEN, M. E.: Relationship between social attitudes toward aging and the delinquencies of youth, presented at the First Pan-American Congress on Gerontology, Mexico City, Sept. 18, 1956. *Am. J. Psychiat., 114*:444-448, 1957.

80. LOWRY, O. H. and HASTINGS, A. B.: Quantitative histochemical changes in aging, in *Cowdry's Problems of Aging,* 3rd Edition, edited by Lansing, A. I., Baltimore, Williams & Wilkins, 1952.

81. MA, C. K. and COWDRY, E. V.: Aging of elastic tissue in human skin. *J. Gerontology, 5*:203-209, 1950.

82. MALAMUD, W.; SANDS, S. L.; MALAMUD, I., and POWERS, P. J. P.: Involutional psychoses. *Am. J. Psychiat., 105*:567, 1949.

83. MALAMUD, W.: Current trends and needs in research on problems of the aged. *Dis. Nerv. System, 2*:37-45, 1941.

84. MALAMUD, W.: The psychopathology of aging, in *The Neurologic and Psychiatric Aspects of the Disorders of Aging.* Baltimore, Williams & Wilkins, 1956.

85. McCAY, C. M.: Chemical aspects of aging and the effect of diet upon aging, in *Cowdry's Problems of Aging,* 3rd Edition, edited by Lansing, A. I. Baltimore, Williams & Wilkins, 1952.

86. MASSERMAN, J. H.: The psychodynamics of aging. *Geriatrics, 12*:115-122, 1957.

87. MASSERMAN, J. H.: Biodynamic therapy in the aging: An integration, in *Progress in Psychotherapy,* edited by Masserman, J. H., and Moreno, J. L. New York, Grune & Stratton, 1957.

88. MEERLOO, J. A. M.: Transference and resistance in geriatric psychotherapy. *Psychoanalyt. Rev., 42*:1, 1955.

89. MILES, W. R.: Correlation of reaction and coordination speed with age in adults. *Am. J. Psychol., 43*: 377, 1931.

90. NIKITIN, W. N.; GOLUBIZKA, and others: The biochemical age change of the denervative organs. *Uchen Zapiski, Kharkov Univ., 68*:79-99, 1956.

91. O'LEARY, J. L.: Aging in the nervous system, in *Cowdry's Problem of Aging*, 3rd Edition, edited by Lansing, A. I. Baltimore, Williams & Wilkins, 1952.

92. OVERHOLSER, W.: Orientation, mental health in later maturity. Suppl. N. 168, U.S. Public Health Reports, 1942.

93. OVERHOLSER, W.: The problem of mental disease in an aging population. National Conf. of Social Work, 1941.

94. PECK, R.: Psychological developments in the second half of life, in *Psychological Aspects of Aging*. Proceedings of a conference on planning research, Bethesda, Md., April 24-27, John E. Anderson, editor. Am. Psychol. Assoc., Washington, D.C., 1955.

95. RICHARDSON, I. M.: Retirement: A Social-Medical study of 244 men. *Scottish M. J., 1*:381-391, Dec., 1956.

96. ROBINSON, S.: Experimental studies of physical fitness in relation to age. *Arbeitsphysiologie, 16*:251-323, 1938.

97. ROBINSON, S.; BRUCER, M.: Range of normal blood pressure. *Arch. Intern. Med., 64*:409-444, 1939.

98. SCHIELE, B. C.: Panel discussion on tranquillizing drugs in the clinical management of mental disease in geriatric patients. The Am. Geriatric Society and The Am. Academy of General Practice, New York City, Nov. 19, 1956.

99. SCHILDER, P.: Psychiatric aspects of old age and aging. The *Am. J. Orthopsychiat., 10*:62-69, 1940.

100. SCHILDER, R.: Introduction to a psychoanalytic psychiatry. Nervous and Mental Disease, Monograph Series, N. 50, 1928.

101. SELYE, H.: The stress of life. New York, McGraw-Hill, 1956.

102. SHOCK, N. W.: Aging of homeostatic mechanisms, in *Cowdry's Problems of Aging,* 3rd Edition, edited by Lansing, A. I. Baltimore, Williams & Wilkins, 1952.

103. SHOCK, N. W.: Age changes in some physiologic processes. *Geriatrics, 12*:40-48, 1957.

104. SHOCK, N. W.: Trends in gerontology, 2nd Edition. Stanford, Stanford University Press, 1957.

105. STARE, F. J.: Nutrition and aging. *J. Am. Geriatrics Soc., 3*:767-777, 1955.

106. STIEGLITZ, E. J.: Principles of geriatrics medicine. In *Geriatric Medicine,* 3rd Edition, edited by Stieglitz, E. J. Philadelphia, Lippincott, 1954.

107. STIEGLITZ, E. J.: Foundation of geriatric medicine, in *Geriatric Medicine,* 3rd Edition, edited by Stieglitz, E. J., Philadelphia, Lippincott, 1954.

108. STIEGLITZ, E. J.: The Second Forty Years. Philadelphia, Lippincott, 1946.

109. STREIB, G. F., and THOMPSON, W. E.: Personal and social adjustment in retirement, in *The New Frontiers of Aging,* edited by W. Donahue and C. Tibbitts. Ann Arbor, The University of Michigan Press, 1957.

110. THEWLIS, M. W.: *The Care of the Aged.* St. Louis, Mosby, 1954.

111. WALLERSTEIN, R. S.: Treatment of the psychosis of general paresis with combined sodium amytal and psychotherapy. *Psychiatry, 14*:307-317, 1951.

112. WECHSLER, D.: The Measurement of Adult Intelligence. Baltimore, Williams & Wilkins, 1951.

113. WEISS, E., and ENGLISH, O. S.: *Psychosomatic Medicine.* Philadelphia, Saunders, 1943.

114. WEXBERG, L. E.: Discussion, in Kolb, 1. "The Psychiatric Significance of Aging as a Public Health Problem" in *Mental Health in Later Maturity.* Federal Security Agency, U.S. Public Health Service, Supplement N. 168, p. 19.

115. WHITE, E. B.: A stratagem for retirement. *Holiday,* March, 1956, pp. 84-87.

116. WOLFF, K.: Sul problema dei tumori. *Morgagni, N.* 27, 1935.

117. WOLFF, K.: Treatment of the geriatric patient in a mental hospital. *J. Am. Geriatrics Soc., 4*:472-476, 1956.

118. WOLFF, K.: Definition of the geriatric patient. *Geriatrics, 12*:102-106, 1957.

119. WOLFF, K.: Group psychotherapy with geriatric patients in a mental hospital, *J. Am. Geriatrics Soc., 5*:13-19, 1957.

120. WOLFF, K.: Occupational therapy for geriatric patients in a mental hospital: therapeutic possibilities and limitations. *J. Am. Geriatrics Soc., 5*:1019-1024, 1957.

121. WOLFF, K.: Psychiatric evaluation of geriatric patients on an outpatient basis: preliminary study. *J. Am. Geriatrics Soc., 6*:760-765, 1958.

122. WOLFF, K.: Active therapy replaces custodial care for geriatric patients in mental hospitals. *Geriatrics, 13*:174-175, 1958.